GODDESS SPELLS
for Busy Girls

GODDESS SPELLS

for Busy Girls

GET RICH, GET HAPPY, GET LUCKY

JEN McCONNEL

WEISER BOOKS
San Francisco, CA / Newburyport, MA

First published in 2014 by Weiser Books

Red Wheel/Weiser, LLC
With offices at:
665 Third Street, Suite 400
San Francisco, CA 94107

www.redwheelweiser.com

ISBN: 978-1-57863-548-1

Library of Congress Cataloging-in-Publication Data available upon request
Cover design by Jim Warner
Interior by Deborah Dutton
Typeset in Warnock Pro Light text and Univers Condensed and
Liberty Display

Printed in the United States of America
MAL

10 9 8 7 6 5 4 3 2 1

The paper used in this publication meets the minimum requirements of
the American National Standard for Information Sciences—Permanence of
Paper for Printed Library Materials Z39.48-1992 (R1997).

CONTENTS

INTRODUCTION

Magic works. For a long time, I didn't believe it. Actually, that's not exactly true. For a long time, I didn't believe that *I* could do magic. I didn't think I was special enough, or skilled enough, or sparkly enough. And then I tried a simple spell that changed my life.

I was attending an herbal workshop one spring, and the smiling instructor spent the morning teaching us which herbs to use for which types of magic. She had us each attempt four spells: one for each of the four elements. Because she had told us that air magic was good for safety and travel, I threw my energy (and a lot of herbs) into a spell that I thought would never come true.

I've always loved to travel, but the one place that filled my dreams since childhood was Egypt. Now, if you've ever looked at plane tickets to Egypt, you know it isn't exactly a walk in the park. At that time, my newly married husband and I had been dreaming about a delayed honeymoon in the land of the pharaohs, but we both knew that it was unlikely to happen anytime soon. *What the heck,* I thought; *I'll do this spell and see if it will help.* I filled a small cotton bag with herbs and a tiny crystal, and I filled myself with the intention to make the trip happen. I didn't try to conjure money with the spell; instead, I just focused on the idea of traveling to the exotic, unknown land of my dreams with my husband beside me.

A month after I made the charm bag, I won enough money in a local raffle to cover the cost of two plane tickets. I didn't hesitate: I knew that money was meant to get me to Egypt, and with some convincing, my eternally practical sweetie agreed. There's no doubt in my mind that the trip manifested due to my simple spell.

Since that time, I've learned to take magic a lot more seriously. Simple spells can yield amazing results, and we don't have to have any special training or initiation to work magic. The ability to transform our lives through magic rests within each of us. This collection of spells will not only allow you to tap into your natural ability, but it will also give you access to the vibrant forces of many goddesses from around the globe.

Goddess magic is powerful magic: with the help of the right goddess, your spell will be imbued with phenomenal strength. Thousands of people over the centuries have sent their dreams and wishes out to various goddesses, and these divine ladies carry the residual spark of years of worship. Working goddess magic is as easy as working magic in general, but you get the extra sparkle that goddesses bring to everything.

The first thing you'll want to do when you decide to work goddess magic is to get to know the different goddesses. This book provides an introduction to twenty-five celestial ladies, but you can always go in search of even more information. Just make sure you are asking the right goddess for help; it would be a bad idea to ask Hecate to intercede in your love life, and an even worse idea to ask Lakshmi to help you defend yourself in a violent situation. Knowing a little bit about the different goddesses will guide your magic and make it easier to choose which lady you want to work with.

Magical Protection

Before attempting any kind of spell, make sure you are prepared. You wouldn't try to drive a car without a hard-earned license, would you? Magical preparation is a bit different than mundane preparation, but you still need to take safety precautions before beginning any spell.

At the very least, you should ground and center before doing spell work. There are a variety of ways to do this, and I'll share four with you right now, plus a more formal way. As an added bonus, you can use these grounding and centering methods even if you aren't about to work magic. Whenever you're feeling frazzled, these will help!

I'M A TREE

Connecting to the earth beneath you is one of the quickest ways to ground and center. Close your eyes while sitting or standing. Imagine that you are a tree (or any other plant that you prefer). Feel the strength of your torso and the life flowing up toward your head. Imagine branches or blossoms shooting out of the crown of your head. Now, feel yourself sending roots down into the earth. The roots anchor you to the earth, but they also sustain you. As your roots reach deeper, you can feel the energy of the planet coursing up and into you, climbing your torso, and spilling down your body. Take at least five deep breaths in this pose, feeling the energy climb from your roots with each inhale. With each exhale, feel the energy of the earth reaching through your branches and surrounding you. When you feel steady, you can open your eyes and begin your spell.

ENTRANCED

Find an instrumental song or chant without distinguishable words. (There are tons of these online, but even your great uncle's classical music CD will work.) Plug in your headphones or lock yourself in a room with the music. Sit down in a comfortable position and close your eyes. Take a deep breath, listening to the music. Try to clear your mind of thoughts and just focus on the sound. Breathe deeply, and keep your eyes closed for three breaths after the music ends. When you open your eyes, you should be ready to work magic.

MERMAID

(*Note:* This is not the best method to ground and center before doing a bath-based spell, unless you want to end up totally pruney.)

Fill your tub with hot water (or, alternately, take a hot shower). Don't use any soap or bubble bath; just immerse yourself in the warmth. Close your eyes and listen to the water flowing or lapping around you. Feel the warmth seeping into your core. When you are warm, calm, and content, you can open your eyes and drain the tub. Once you're dry, you'll be ready to start your spell.

SPARKLER

Find a comfortable, dark place to sit. Bring a blanket or a warm sweater, and snuggle in. Light a candle and set it in front of you (being careful to observe good fire safety habits). Stare into the flame. Try to empty your mind; ignore any fleeting thoughts that may pass through it. Just watch the candle and breathe. Take at least fifteen deep breaths while watching the candle. When you feel still and calm, you can blow out the candle and begin your spell.

CASTING A CIRCLE

If you want to do something a little more formal than just a simple grounding and centering exercise before you work magic, you might consider casting a circle. Ground and center with whichever method you prefer, and then begin to cast your circle.

Casting a circle is a way of creating formal, sacred space wherever you are. It sets your magical work apart from the mundane world and provides you with psychic protection as you cast your spells. Some people like to use particular tools to cast a circle, such as an athame, a wand, or a braid of burning sage, but in its most basic form, all you need is yourself.

To cast a simple circle, first make sure you've assembled all the tools you will need for your spell. You don't want to break the circle by running back and forth to get things after you've already begun. Once you ground and center, stand in the middle of the space that will be your circle. Face the four quarters, starting with either north or east, depending on your preference, and invite each quarter to protect you. You can make up quarter calls, or you can say something like this:

To the north, powers of earth, I ask your aid.
To the east, powers of air, I ask your aid.
To the south, powers of fire, I ask your aid.
To the west, powers of water, I ask your aid.

The next step in casting a circle is to invite the assistance of a deity. If you are about to do a spell with the assistance of a particular goddess, now would be a great time to call her. You might say:

Athena, please be with me today and always.

Once you've called the quarters and whichever deity or deities you wish, your circle is complete. You can add elaborate ritual to the process, but if you're in a rush, a simple circle will work just fine. Feel free to adapt the process to better suit your individual practice.

Tools

All of the spells in this book are designed to be simple. You can usually complete each one with items you have on hand, but here are a few things you might want to add to your shopping list:

- **Spell candles, all colors.** These are small candles, about half an inch in diameter and four inches tall. Most New Age stores sell them, but if you aren't near any such shops, check your local, organic grocery store. You can also order them online for a fairly reasonable price.

- **Olive oil.** Generally speaking, you can use most edible oils as a base for spells, but I prefer olive oil (and some goddesses, such as Athena, prefer it, too).

- **Essential oil.** Another product you can usually find at an organic grocery store is essential oils. These can be expensive, and they are usually optional when doing spells. Just note that the expense can be worth it: cinnamon oil in particular adds quite a punch to your spells.

- **A journal.** It's a good idea to keep a dedicated magical notebook, not just for the spells that demand writing, but to reflect on your experiences with each spell and goddess as well. Buy something beautiful, and use it as part of your magic.

- **Herbs.** All of the herbs mentioned in these spells are the ones most of us have in our pantries. Fresh herbs are often better for spell work (unless dry is specified), but I've been known to use the same dried, powdered herbs that I cook with for magic. Whatever works for you is fine!

  Just read the list of ingredients carefully before beginning any spell. You'll be surprised at how many magical tools you already have on hand!

Magical Ethics

No book of magic would be complete without a brief discussion of magical ethics. When working magic, it's important to remember two things: every human being is unique, and every human being has free will. For those reasons, I try to only cast spells that affect my own life, and I never cast spells that interfere with another person's choices, mostly because I would hate to have my own choices taken away. You must develop your own personal code of ethics when it comes to magic, just as you must come to your own conclusions in your mundane life. Whatever path you follow, think long and hard about free will and individuality before casting any spell.

How to Use This Book

I know you're dying to start casting spells, but just in case you were wondering, there are a few ways to approach this book.

BY ISSUE

Chapters 1 through 5 are structured around common issues. Chapter 1 deals with health and wellness, both mental and physical. Chapter 2 deals with interpersonal relationships, including those with family, friends, and lovers. Chapter 3 deals with hearth and home, offering suggestions for ways you can make any space secure. In chapter 4, spells for travel and protection are introduced. Chapter 5 focuses on all forms of abundance and fortune. Then, chapter 6 offers suggestions for group magic, which can be an exciting way to shake up your magical practice. And chapter 7 is filled with spells of gratitude, so when you're done changing your life, you can make sure you stop and give thanks!

BY GODDESS

Do you want to know more about Isis? Maybe you've always had a thing for Aphrodite. Each of the twenty-five goddesses in this book has three spells associated with her, so you can use this book as a way to develop a deeper relationship with the goddess of your choice. Read her myth, work through her spells, and journal about your experience. You never know; you might find your next patron!

IN A GROUP

Chapter 6 focuses on adapting the spells in this book for work with a group. It also includes a list of suggestions for rituals and gatherings focused on goddess magic. If you and a group of friends would like to use this book together, chapter 6 is the place to begin.

What are you waiting for? It's time to meet some goddesses and start making magic!

CHAPTER 1

Don't Forget to Take Your (Magic) Vitamins!

Once a week, I attend an intense and satisfying yoga class with a friend. I am comfortable there: I place my mat in the back, near the windows, and I breathe as evenly as I can, content that no one is judging or observing me.

But last summer, I stepped away from the studio. I made plans to meet a friend and carpool to the local minor league baseball park, where our community was convening for an hour of outdoor yoga practice. The thought of trying something new with the support of a trusted friend wasn't daunting, and I cheerfully got up early on a Saturday morning. I was just finishing breakfast when I heard from my friend. She was ill, and wouldn't be joining me.

To be honest, I seriously considered staying home. Without the security of a known companion, I wasn't sure I wanted to enter such a large group of strangers. What if they were are truly serious yogis, and what if they realized that I was still very much a beginner? What if everyone there was skinnier than I was?

As my thoughts spun and I prepared to give up on attending, another what-if changed my mind. What if I didn't go? As soon as I voiced the thought, my spirits fell. I really wanted to attend this event, so despite my nerves, I grabbed my green yoga mat and headed downtown.

When I surged with the crowd onto the grassy outfield, I spread my mat close to a row of women and sat down, trying to find my center before beginning the practice. My eyes kept flickering open, though, and I found myself watching the people around me. Young, old, in between like me, there were men and women of every shape and size. Gradually, I began to relax.

Once the practice began, I melted into the community. We raised our arms to the heavens together, breathing deeply and enjoying the fresh air and warm sunshine. The "om" at the end of practice was the most amazing thing: it was like a hive of bees, pulsing and buzzing together. Laying back in corpse pose, a thought filled my heart and exploded into my body. It's not about me, I realized; it's about we.

As women, we tend to run out of time or energy when it comes to caring for ourselves. Work, family, school, everything stacks up in importance, bumping little old you down to the bottom of the list. And let's face it: things that end up that far down the list rarely get tackled.

The spells in this section address three aspects of being well: there are spells for health in times of sickness, spells for memory retention and clarity of thought, and spells to help you connect with your own divine nature. Athena, the first goddess of this chapter, is a great partner when you are seeking a clear mind. Sekhmet will help you heal your body, while Amaterasu rules body image and feelings of worth. Work with Sarasvati to infuse your life with beauty, and call on Oya when you just need to be purified. Remember to approach each deity with respect, and be prepared to listen to her teachings.

Athena

Titles: Grey-Eyed One, Lady of Snakes, Pallas Athena

Attributes: Wisdom, Council, Judgment, Strength, Battle

Colors: White, Gray, Blue

Animals: Owl, Snake

Culture of Origin: Pre-Greek, Hellenistic

Although she's one powerful goddess, Athena's traditional followers didn't include a lot of women. She tended to favor flawed, foxy heroes like Odysseus while changing uppity girls like Arachne into spiders. But that doesn't mean you should ignore this motherless goddess: Athena values knowledge, and she's willing to assist those who are genuine in their search for understanding. Do not, under any circumstance, make the mistake of calling on this goddess to help in matters of the heart: Athena may be queen of the mind, but when it comes to relationships, her track record isn't exactly glistening.

Athena was born in an unusual way, even for a goddess. In the Greek version of her myth, she is the child of the king of the gods, although there is some evidence that she predates the Hellenistic culture. This story is the most well-known and has become the most associated with Athena's conception.

Her father, Zeus, was a bit of a ladies' man, and even though he'd been warned not to, he hooked up with Metis, the crafty goddess of thought and wisdom. Afterward, he was hit with remorse and worry: what if this goddess bore a son who would destroy him? To keep that from happening, Zeus swallowed the woman. He thought trouble had been averted, but then the headaches started. Zeus was in so much pain that he finally had to ask his blacksmith son, Hephaestus, to crack open his skull. Out popped Athena, fully grown and clothed in beautiful armor. This fierce and unexpected goddess instantly became the favorite child of Zeus.

Athena is not just another figure of war: her armor signifies protection and thoughtful confrontation, rather than hotheaded combat. As a goddess who never took a lover, Athena is viewed as a perpetual maiden, wise beyond imagining but without the chains that sometimes hamper goddesses who are tied to men. She values honesty, wisdom, and clear thought, and if you approach her for help in any of these areas, you will find her willing to listen.

This is also a goddess who is familiar with disappointment. She went up against Hera and Aphrodite to compete for the title of the fairest, most worthy goddess. Not only would the winner get the glory, she would also get an enchanted golden apple. Competition between the goddesses was fierce. Their judge, the mortal prince of Troy named Paris, couldn't decide. Each goddess offered him a bribe hoping to sway his vote, and he foolishly spurned Athena's offer to become the wisest ruler the earth had ever known. Instead, he awarded Aphrodite the apple and collected his prize: a girl named Helen who was already married to another guy. Although she was bitterly disappointed, Athena didn't sulk and whine: she backed the Greeks when they waged war on Troy and got even with Paris. I'm sure you know how that story turned out: it took ten years, but eventually, Athena felt that her slight had been repaid. This is not a goddess you want to cross!

When working with this goddess for clarity and better judgment, do not expect things to happen quickly. Athena's wisdom is passed on slowly and only as you are ready: nothing with this goddess will occur in the blink of an eye. Be patient and tell her truthfully what you seek, and if she believes you truly need it, Athena will come to your aid.

SPELL FOR MEMORY RETENTION

This spell is ideal when you are working on a test or project that requires a clear head with facts and figures at your disposal.

YOU WILL NEED

- Olive oil
- A small jar with a lid
- Basil leaves
- A lemon
- A bathtub

1. Pour the olive oil into a small jar. (The kind you cook with is fine or whatever is on hand. Athena appreciates practicality.) You don't need more than a cup, and less is fine, too.

2. Into this jar, put:
   Five basil leaves (preferably fresh, but dried is fine)
   A slice of lemon (feel free to squeeze the lemon juice and save it for later)

3. Seal the jar and give it a few swift shakes. While the jar is sitting, run a cool bath. (Not so cold that you can't stand it, but not too hot: aim for just below room temperature.)

4. While the water is running, pour half the contents of the jar into the bath. Ease yourself into the water and empty your mind. Feel your thoughts swirling around you like the water. Watch the way the oil collects on the surface, making patterns.

5. When the bath is as full as you would like, shut off the water and sit in silence for a few minutes. Contemplate what you are asking Athena for: why do you need help with your memory?

6. When you feel that your thoughts are orderly, speak your request aloud to Athena. *"I ask you, great Athena, for clarity of thought. Help me to retain these facts _____ so that I might honor you with wisdom in this situation _____."*

7. Anoint your temples and your third eye with some of the remaining oil. When you drain the bath, pour what's left of the oil over your feet as you stand in the tub. Seal the spell by saying, *"Like you, Athena, I hope to walk in wisdom."*

8. It's fine to shower after this spell if you don't like the oily residue on your skin; Athena won't mind.

SPELL FOR CLEAR THINKING

Use this spell anytime you are feeling cloudy or muddled. When the charm breaks, don't repair it: burn it, and make a new one.

YOU WILL NEED

- Five strands of thread, about three times as long as your ankle (You can use yarn, ribbon, twine, hemp, or embroidery floss. I prefer embroidery floss or hemp, but whatever is on hand is perfectly fine.)

1. Tie one end of the threads together with a knot. Spread the threads out so you can see each one (this helps if the threads are each a different color.)

2. Take the far left thread and tie one knot around the thread beside it. Still using the same thread, tie a knot on each successive thread, moving from left to right. The far left thread has now become the far right thread.

3. Repeat this process. As you begin to find a rhythm in your work, let your hands take over. Speak words like *"clarity," "thought," "intelligence," "wisdom," "free," "light,"* and any other words that spring to mind when you think of clear, level thinking. You might find yourself repeating words, and your speech may slip into a chant. Don't question yourself: whatever you are doing or saying is exactly right. Athena listens to the words of the heart rather than to prepared speeches.

4. Eventually, the thread will begin to resemble a small weaving. Keep tying knots, left to right, moving the thread across and starting with the next thread, until you've created something that looks a bit like the friendship bracelets girls still make.

5. When you are done, knot the loose threads in one knot at the end of the weaving. Tie it around your right ankle, and snip any threads that are too long.

6. Once you are wearing your charm, stand up with your legs spread shoulder-width. Raise your arms above you in a strong V, like a gymnast taking a bow. Seal the spell by saying, *"Through my hands, clear thought and wisdom come to me. Blessed be, Athena, Lady of Snakes."* (The snake has long been seen as a symbol of wisdom around the world, and some of Athena's ancient images show her with snakes at her feet and upon her shoulders.)

7. Know that as you walk through your day, the wisdom of your fingers is working in your mind. When the charm breaks or falls off, burn it and give thanks to Athena. If you still feel that you are lacking in clear thought, make another one, but wait at least a week after the original charm is finished doing its work: you never know what may happen between spells!

SPELL TO ELIMINATE SELF-JUDGMENT

We all have a voice inside that compares us to others. Silence that voice with Athena's help.

YOU WILL NEED

- An apple
- A knife
- A surface appropriate for cutting

1. First, listen to the voice of self-doubt in your mind. Let her hurl her slings and arrows: feel the sting of each insult.

2. When she's worn herself out, slice the apple horizontally across the core. You will see a five-pointed star inside the fruit when you do this.

3. Offer half of the apple to Athena. Say, *"Mighty Athena, I know that you are filled with great worth. I give you this apple as a token of the respect you are due."* (Leave this half of the apple outside, or if that isn't possible, bury it in a houseplant.)

4. Prepare to eat the other half of the apple. Before you do, say, *"Athena, I ask that you take away my negative perceptions. Let me view the beauty and power that I possess without criticism. Help me to love my flawed self."* Eat your half of the apple.

5. Seal the spell by saying, *"Thanks to you, Athena, I will no longer judge myself harshly. I am a woman of strength and intelligence, and like you, I will walk proud."*

Sekhmet

Titles: Eye of Ra, The Destroyer, Great Mother, Lady of Pestilence

Attributes: Battle, Destruction, Protection, Solar Deity

Colors: Red, Orange, Yellow

Animals: Lioness, Cat, Cow

Culture of Origin: Egypt

While the images of Sekhmet that have survived into the modern era hold a certain kind of serenity, this goddess is anything but passive. Sekhmet is the battle form of the great cow goddess, Hathor (we'll discuss her later on), and as such, she is depicted with a female body and the head of a regal lioness. Her breasts are proudly bared, and her feline smile makes you think she knows a secret . . . or she just ate a herd of gazelles.

In her primary myth, Sekhmet is an unrestrained force of rage. When the sun god Ra grew weary of the people on the earth, he called on Sekhmet to rid him of their lazy, destructive ways. You don't have to ask this goddess for help twice: she immediately came to earth and began flattening everything in her path. Everywhere she looked, she saw people who didn't respect the gods, and as her anger grew, she started to enjoy the slaughter.

As Ra and the other gods watched her, they became increasingly worried that they wouldn't be able to curb her enthusiasm for destruction. The sun god had a change of heart and decided at the eleventh hour that he wanted to spare the human race, but he was frightened of the goddess he had unleashed. He called all the gods together to discuss the problem, and they finally concocted a plan to stop Sekhmet. If it worked, humanity would be saved. If it didn't, well, the goddess might turn her wrath on the rest of her pantheon. Despite the risk, the gods took the plunge and crossed their fingers.

The gods brewed a huge vat of beer and colored it with crushed ocher. When they poured the beer out in Sekhmet's path, it looked like the ground was bathed in blood. Battle lust overcame her, and she fell to her knees, lapping up the crimson booze. It was only when she had drunk it all that she forgot about the destruction of humanity. Drunk and docile, she transformed back into lowing Hathor, and the gods breathed a sigh of relief.

Although this myth might seem to portray Sekhmet as something to be feared or mocked, there is strength at the heart of this tale. Sekhmet is a good reminder that even the kindest and quietest woman has the strength of a lioness within her. This goddess may not burst forth very often, but when she makes her presence known, the world trembles.

Despite her attempted destruction of humanity, the ancient Egyptians worshiped Sekhmet as the patron of surgeons and healing. Her statues once lined the border of Egypt, and it's been suggested that pharaohs would occasionally have her images dusted with poisonous spores to infect any invading armies that came by. Whether this is true or not, Sekhmet is inextricably linked to health and is an ideal goddess to invoke when working on your physical body. Her aid is swift, and sometimes larger than expected: working magic with Sekhmet indicates that you are 110 percent committed to the change you seek. She never does anything halfway, and she expects the same thing from the people who call upon her.

Resist the temptation to do the following spells for minor ailments: seek out Sekhmet in times of real illness, and she will answer your call with fierceness and speed. A cold can be dealt with without magic, but if you are facing the flu, for example, you need all the help you can get. Charms for everyday wellness can invoke this goddess, but remember to keep the lines of communication open: this is not a one-way goddess. If she feels unappreciated, her legendary rage may surface. Always, always, always remember to say thank you! Be specific when working with this goddess, and let her fierce heat fill you with health.

SPELL FOR PREVENTING ILLNESS

Whenever you feel vulnerable to illness, whether it's due to a change in the weather, travel plans, or unhealthy work conditions, spend a few minutes each morning on this spell. The more you do it, the better you will feel!

YOU WILL NEED

- Some uninterrupted time

1. First thing in the morning, before you shower or even brush your teeth, stand and face the south. Close your eyes and raise your hands above your head, standing in the shape of a Y. Visualize the red-hot glow of the sun on your face. Feel the heat washing over you, making your skin prickle as if you are about to get a bad sunburn. Let the heat fill you.

2. When you are warmed to the core, repeat this chant at least nine times: *"Sekh-met."* Clip your words, making each syllable sharp and distinct. As you chant, gradually increase your volume.

3. When you feel the vibration of the words deep in your chest, draw your hands together over your head and pull them slowly down the front of your body, coming to rest in a prayer in front of your heart center, right between your breasts. Stop chanting.

4. Keep breathing slowly and steadily, feeling the heat of fire flow through your body. When you open your eyes, keep your hands at your heart and bow to the south.

5. Repeat this spell daily as needed.

SPELL FOR REMOVING ILLNESS

Sometimes, all the preventive measures in the world can't stop sickness. When you fall ill, let Sekhmet's fire heal your body.

YOU WILL NEED

- A small spell candle (red, orange, or yellow)
- A needle or another pointed object
- Cinnamon oil
- A mirror
- Matches

1. Invoke Sekhmet before you begin. Say, *"Goddess Sekhmet, Lady of Pestilence, I ask that you take away my physical ailments. Give me health, great Lady, so that I can live well."* Repeat this nine times.

2. Using a needle or a pencil or something else with a point, carve symbols or words that represent your illness onto the candle. You can use only one symbol, or you can cover the candle. Be specific, and follow your instinct.

3. Anoint the candle with the cinnamon oil. If you have sensitive skin, you can skip this step, but the oil adds potency to this spell.

4. Set the candle on top of the mirror. Before you light it, look down into your face reflected from the mirror. Visualize whatever it is that ails you, and allow yourself to fully inhabit the pain and discomfort for a moment. As you light the candle, visualize what it will be like when you are healed. Watch your face and the flame for a moment, but be careful not to come too close to the fire: we don't want you getting burned instead of healed!

5. You can either stay and meditate in front of the candle, or you can leave it and go about your day. If you leave it, make sure it is somewhere safe that won't be disturbed by pets or family members. Let the candle burn down: do not extinguish it.

6. If your space allows, keep the mirror somewhere that you will see it each day. Look into the glass and know that Sekhmet is working on your problem.

SPELL TO INCREASE PHYSICAL ENERGY

Sometimes, we all feel a little run-down. Ask Sekhmet to recharge you whenever your battery is drained.

YOU WILL NEED

- A small stone (tiger's-eye, red agate, or amber)
- A piece of tinfoil

1. Take the stone and set it on the tinfoil. Leave this somewhere in direct sunlight to charge. Make sure you don't forget about the spell: you want solar energy for this, not lunar, so you need to complete the spell within one day.

2. Before the sun sets, take the stone and cup it between your hands as if you are clapping. Imagine that you are holding a tiny sun. Lift the stone to your lips and blow on it gently, infusing it with your energy. Say, *"Sekhmet, Eye of Ra, as you wear the energy of the sun upon your brow, let me too carry the sun with me. This stone is my sun."* Repeat this invocation three times.

3. Touch the stone to your forehead, just above your eyebrows. Say, *"My solar crown is my radiance. I am radiant. I am energy. I am fire."*

4. Cup the stone again between your hands, holding it in front of your heart center. Bow to Sekhmet, and thank her for her help. Carry the stone with you whenever you need an energy boost. Make sure you don't bring it into the bedroom with you at night so you can sleep soundly!

Amaterasu

Titles: Imperial Mother, Shining One in Heaven, Lady of Light

Attributes: Mirrors, Self-Knowing, Power, Protection, Blessing, Weaving, Solar Deity

Colors: White, Gold, Yellow

Animals: Horse, Sparrow, Finch, and Other Songbirds

Culture of Origin: Japan

Like Sekhmet, Amaterasu is a solar goddess, but she's fierce in a much less obvious way than the lioness. Amaterasu is the primary goddess in the Shinto faith, and she is considered the throne-mother of the imperial family of Japan. This solar goddess lived peacefully in heaven for a time, but a conflict with her feisty brother, the god of storms Susanoo, drove her into hiding for a brief period. Don't assume she's a weak or easily frightened goddess: wait until you hear what her nasty brother did to her.

Susanoo and Amaterasu were, like so many siblings, constantly struggling over who was the best. After one of their arguments, Susanoo decided to get back at Amaterasu. He trashed her celestial weaving room, killed one of her sacred horses, and murdered her favorite handmaiden as well. He thought this would demonstrate his strength and superiority once and for all, but his plan backfired.

Furious with her brother, Amaterasu locked herself inside a deep cave, taking the nourishment and light of the sun with her. The world was plunged into darkness. While she hid in the cave, she mourned the losses she had suffered and waited for her brother to properly apologize. But the apology never came.

Frantic for their livelihoods and the lives of the mortals on earth, the other gods gathered outside Amaterasu's cave and begged her to show herself. The goddess would not relent. Her stubborn brother would not say he was sorry, and so she would not come out of the darkness. For a time, the gods were at a loss, until the tricky, bawdy goddess Uzume devised a plan.

Uzume instructed the other gods to fashion a large mirror, which they hung from a tree directly outside of Amaterasu's cave. Then, Uzume began to dance and tell jokes. The goddess of dance and mirth pranced about, entertaining the gods with increasingly bawdy and ridiculous dance moves, and their laughter penetrated Amaterasu's cave. Alone in the darkness, she began to wonder what was taking place out in the world, and gradually, her curiosity overcame her rage.

When Amaterasu peeked around the entrance to her cave, she immediately caught sight of her own radiant reflection in the large mirror. The goddess was captivated: she had never seen herself before, and as she gazed in wonder at her beauty, Uzume pulled her out of the cave. The other gods sealed it behind her, preventing Amaterasu from ever leaving them again.

At first glance, this myth seems to tell us that the goddess is weak and vain, but I think Amaterasu is stronger than that. This goddess is extremely proud and self-aware: she knows her own value, which is why her pride never allows her to back down from the conflict with her pesky brother. She also understands her strength, and by depriving the world of her light, she silently proves to her brother and the other gods how much they truly need her. And when faced with her beautiful reflection for the first time, this goddess doesn't simper or act coy; she falls into worshipful love with herself.

We can learn a lot from Amaterasu about self-love and the power that comes from it. The spells in this section are designed to help you know and value yourself. As Amaterasu shows us, if you aren't aware of your own worth, no one else will be able to see your light. But when we pass through each day in true self-awareness, others crave our unique brilliance.

SPELL FOR SELF-AWARENESS

Before we can love ourselves, we must know ourselves intimately. Use this spell to Amaterasu on each new moon to listen to the changes within yourself.

YOU WILL NEED

- A blank journal (Dedicate a specific journal just for this spell, and each time you repeat the spell, you can look back at yourself.)
- A large yellow candle
- Something to write with (I prefer a purple ballpoint pen.)

1. This spell is best timed to the new moon or the nights closely surrounding it. Sit in a darkened room with your journal closed on your lap. Let your breathing adjust until you feel your heartbeat become steady.

2. Light the yellow candle, and place it in front of you, saying, *"Amaterasu, Lady of Light, shine your mirror upon my soul."*

3. Ask yourself this question (out loud or silently): *"Who am I in this moment?"*

4. Start writing any words, phrases, or titles that spring to mind. Don't judge what comes out on the paper: just keep writing.

5. When you feel that you have nothing more to say, read what you've just written out loud. Again, this isn't about judging your answers: read them with a detached eye, as if they are merely words.

6. How does your list make you feel? Write down your thoughts and emotions connected to the soul work you just did. When you've processed everything and have nothing left to say, mark the page in your journal and close it. Leave it in a safe, dark place until the next new moon.

7. Extinguish the candle, saying *"Thanks be to Amaterasu for this moment of clarity. With your help, I hope to see myself truly."*

8. Repeat this spell every month. Once every three months, look back at your earlier writings.

SPELL FOR SELF-LOVE

Sometimes, it's hard to love ourselves. Turn to Amaterasu when you need a boost of self-love.

YOU WILL NEED
- Vanilla oil or vanilla-scented perfume
- A small mirror

1. Sit somewhere comfortable. Using the vanilla oil, anoint your throat on either side of the jaw and your heart chakra. Rub your hands together quickly, dispelling any remaining oil into your palms. Keep rubbing your hands until you feel warmth and tingling.

2. When your hands are heated, pick up the mirror, keeping it facedown. Say, *"Amaterasu, I want to follow in your footsteps. Help me to love what I see in this glass."*

3. Slowly, turn the mirror over. Cup it in your hands and gradually lift the glass to your face. As you look at yourself, repeat this chant: *"Blessed be the eyes of the goddess that see through me. Blessed be the mouth of the goddess. Blessed be the face of the goddess, for I am she and she is me."*

4. Hold the mirror increasingly closer and allow your gaze to go soft. Love whatever you see.

5. When you are done, set the mirror facedown in a place where it won't be disturbed. Stand and bow to the mirror with your hands pressed into a prayer at your heart, and say, *"I am the goddess, and she is me. I give thanks for my beauty."*

6. Repeat this spell whenever you feel your self-image slipping. Remember, you are a goddess!

SPELL FOR PROTECTION FROM FEAR

Let's face it: sometimes, people or circumstances frighten us. If you feel like your fear is holding you back, try this spell and move forward with joy in your heart.

YOU WILL NEED

- A white candle
- Matches
- An object found outside (A feather is best, but a stone or twig will work, too.)

1. Sit in a comfortable position in the dark. Take three deep breaths, focusing on your inhalation. Light the white candle, saying, *"Amaterasu, woman of strength, shelter me with your loving rays."*

2. Focus on the candle's flame. Imagine that the flame grows slowly and steadily with each breath you take, until the only thing you can see is radiant light. Feel the warmth of the light encircle you, dancing down your

spine, caressing your arms, and settling to the floor like a sheer curtain. When you feel safe and protected, pick up your object.

3. Hold the object in your left hand, and allow yourself to think of the thing which frightens you. See it, hear it, taste it, touch it, and smell it: do not shy away from the fear, but allow yourself to fully experience it.

4. Now, pass the object to your right hand. As you do so, say, *"I transform my fear. It has no form, and cannot harm me."* Visualize the white light that surrounds you being absorbed into the object that you now hold in your right hand.

5. Channel all of the protective energy into your object. It may begin to pulse or glow. Fill it with white light, and when there is only the candle flame left of the light that surrounded you, extinguish the candle, saying, *"May Amaterasu keep my fears small. The light of the goddess shelters me in every moment."*

6. Keep the object as a reminder of the way you have transformed your fear into light.

Repeat this spell only when you face a crippling fear that is negatively impacting your life. This is a powerful spell, and not all fears need to be dealt with in this way.

arasvati

Titles: Learned One, Lady of Art, Brahma's Shakti,
Lady of Letters

Attributes: Art, Creativity, Writing, Music, Beauty,
Learning, Knowledge

Colors: White, Yellow, Gold

Animals: Swan, Goose (Hamsa)

Culture of Origin: India

Wait a minute. You're probably wondering what a goddess of creativity is doing in the health and wellness section of this book, but hang on for a second. True, Sarasvati is the original creative diva: she is said to have invented writing, and she's a patron of all things artistic. But what does that have to do with health?

Plenty! Even if you don't consider yourself a creative person, it's vital that we each have an outlet for our energy to maintain health: otherwise, things get bottled up inside and we turn into a living pressure cooker. Enter Sarasvati, a goddess who remembers to let her feelings out regularly. In fact, one might even say she's free-flowing.

In the earliest myths, Sarasvati is a river goddess, but later on, she loses her watery aspect and steps into a solid female form. In most stories, this crafty goddess is the wife of Brahma, the creator god in the Hindu pantheon. Isn't it interesting that the wife of the top dog, er, god, is not a warrior or an eternal mother, but a craftswoman? Her placement in the mythological hierarchy shows how much importance her earliest worshipers placed on the arts.

Even her conception shows the vital, explosive nature of creativity: if there is no outlet, an idea will create one. At the start of the world, Brahma was content, but he eventually became consumed with loneliness. His loneliness took form, and his body divided into two beings, producing Sarasvati as his literal other half. When she sprang into being, Brahma suddenly gave in to the need to create, and the animals and life on the planet took shape. Without Sarasvati, who knows what kind of world Brahma would have made?

Unlike some of the Hindu deities (we'll talk about Lakshmi later on), Sarasvati does not require much from her followers. She'd rather watch you craft something true than accept offerings of jewels and spices (although she's said to be fond of white flowers), and the greatest way you can connect with this goddess is not through prayers and chanting, but by giving in to the deep creative impulses that wait within. You might say you're not a creative person, but that's ridiculous: every being has the ability to create, and every soul has something beautiful that wants to be expressed.

Call on Sarasvati when you are struggling to express your truest self. Let this goddess guide your hand as you make your mark upon the world, and revel in the joy of creation just for the sake of yourself. Bottling up positive or negative emotions can be detrimental over time. Let Sarasvati help you find an appropriate outlet.

SPELL TO SPARK CREATIVITY

Sometimes, you just need a little push.

YOU WILL NEED

- An orange

1. Take your orange to a sunny spot. This can be inside by a window or outside. Wherever you are, make sure you aren't going to be disturbed.

2. Hold the orange between both hands before your heart center. Think about what creativity means to you. Is it about visual art? Writing? Dancing? Artfully arranging the throw pillows on your couch? There are infinite definitions of creativity, and sometimes we get confused when we are seeking our own. Don't judge the thoughts that pass through your mind: whatever creativity means to you is right.

3. Begin to peel the orange. Go slowly. Keep thinking about your definition of creativity.

4. When the orange is peeled, break off a section. Offer it to Sarasvati, saying, *"Help me find my creativity, Lady of Art."* Leave the orange slice outside for the animals (or throw it outside as soon as you complete the spell).

5. Eat the rest of the orange slice by slice, each time saying, *"I ingest the creative fire of Sarasvati."*

6. When you are done, tackle whatever task you like. You are now infused with creativity, but remember, that doesn't necessarily mean you're going to paint a masterpiece. Trust that Sarasvati is working within you, and trust whatever you do next.

SPELL FOR POSITIVE PROCRASTINATION

Yes, sometimes it's okay to procrastinate. Use this spell to take a creative break without "wasting" time or energy.

YOU WILL NEED

- A notebook
- Something to write with

1. Use this spell if you are feeling stymied and can't help checking Facebook a zillion times when you want to be working.

2. First, turn off your computer. That goes for handheld devices like smartphones and CrackBerries, too. Power down, disconnect the Internet, step into a dark closet. Do whatever you need to focus on the notebook and your pen.

3. Start doodling. The only rule: You have to keep the tip of your pen touching the paper and moving the entire time you recite this charm: *"Sarasvati, Lady of Letters, lend me your thoughts and help me to get beyond distraction. I want to get back to the work at hand, but I want to be*

receptive and ready to create. Sarasvati, Lady of Art, lend me your letters."

4. On the same page as your never-ending doodle, start writing. Just write down anything that comes to mind: why you're mad at your boss, or that annoying thing your boyfriend just said. Hey, look, the cat's taking a nap; that looks nice! Just keep writing until you fill the page. Spelling, grammar, and meaning don't count.

5. Once the page is filled, flip to a clean sheet. Make a list of three things you have to do before the day is over. Only three! No cheating.

6. Now, make a list of three things you want to do.

7. Write out this promise as it applies to you (a, b, and c are the things you *want* to do, while d, e, and f are the *have-tos*.): *"Before I go to bed, I will do a, b, and c. I will also do d, e, and f. This is my promise to Sarasvati."*

8. Put the notebook away and get back to work.

SPELL FOR INSPIRATION

Sometimes, no matter how much we want to create, we feel stymied. Ask Sarasvati for help and watch your talents unfold!

YOU WILL NEED

- A bowl of water
- A small white spell candle

- Matches
- A white flower

1. Sit in a quiet, dark space with the bowl on the ground in front of you. Close your eyes and breathe deeply, clearing your mind with each exhale. Inhale for a count of three, then hold your breath for a count of three. Next, exhale for a count of three, and remain still for a count of three. Repeat this breathing pattern three times.

2. Open your eyes. Light the candle, saying, *"Sarasvati, Lady of Art, I need your help. May my thoughts flow freely like your sacred river. Lady of Letters, let my creativity awaken within me."*

3. Watch the candle flame flicker. Think about the things you want to do: have you always wanted to paint? What about an instrument: do you play one? Hum quietly to yourself as you watch the candle. You can hum any tune, or just buzz tunelessly. Just keep making noise.

4. Set the white flower into the bowl of water. Get your fingertips wet, and flick a little water onto your forehead.

5. Say, *"My thoughts flow like water. Sarasvati is my inspiration."* Repeat this three times.

6. Move the candle to a safe place where it can continue to burn. I like to set mine on my desk when I dive back into my writing, but wherever you stash it, be safe: setting your home on fire is one way to ruin creativity! Don't extinguish this candle, but let it burn itself out.

$\mathcal{O}_{ya}$

Titles: Mother of Nine, Lady of Storms

Attributes: Wind, Storms, Creativity, Rainbows, Weaving, Transitions (Including Death)

Colors: Black, Bright Rainbow Hues

Animal: Goat

Culture of Origin: West African Diaspora

When Oya dances, tornadoes form. With all the bizarre weather patterns in recent years, it's easy to be frightened of this powerful goddess, but the storms she controls are only part of her tale. Oya is a primary Orisha, one of the spirits who originated in West Africa, survived the middle crossing, and became amalgamated with a saint (in her case, the Virgin Mary) in the slave quarters of the Caribbean. It's challenging to parse out Oya's "old-world" attributes when faced with her continuing worship, but that's just another mark of this lady's extreme power.

Oya is the Lady of Storms, but she's also a goddess of craftspeople and merchants. Oya's winds will clear away the cobwebs in your creative life, and she stirs people to take risks in the whirlwind of inspiration. While some consider her to be one of the first Orishas (the area of West Africa where her worship originated is sometimes referred to as "Oya"), it's her later identity that we are going talk about.

Wed to Shango, the king-turned-deity in charge of lightning and firestorms, Oya is more than a match for her temperamental husband. It is said that she challenged him to a magical competition, and despite his self-assurance, she won. Some say that's how she earned her title Mother of Nine; Shango splintered her into nine pieces in anger, and the nine parts of Oya became his daughters.

A version which explores her creative aspect (and, frankly, is a nicer story) attributes her motherhood to self-regeneration. Oya had in her keeping a magical cloth, made of all the colors of the rainbow and imbued with infinite creativity. One day, she cut the cloth, transforming it into her nine precious daughters, who would bear her company when her husband was with his other wives.

Multitalented Oya also has associations with the passage between life and death, and although she is not an underworld figure, she would be a good goddess to work with if you want to strengthen your connection to your ancestors and beloved dead. Is there anything this goddess can't do?

Actually, yes. She can't hold your hand until you become gradually ready for change. Oya is maternal, make no mistake about that, but she's more like the mama bird who pushes her babies out of the nest before they think they are ready. If you decide to work with Oya, expect change: it will be as swift and powerful as her whirling skirts, and equally as unexpected. She'll help you clear away the trash, but she might also clear away things you aren't ready to lose. Still, if you're seeking transformation, especially in terms of your creativity, Oya's your girl.

The spells in this section are diverse, just like this goddess. Work with Oya to remove blocks to your creativity, and let her help you bridge the gap that rests between the living and the dead. Finally, consider Oya an excellent companion when you are seeking empowerment: she's fierce and she knows it, but she's more than willing to help you tap into your own internal tornado. Get ready to be transformed: Oya doesn't do anything by half!

SPELL TO REMOVE CREATIVE BLOCKS

When you feel stymied and you need something that's stronger than a shot of espresso, call on Oya to remove your creative blocks.

YOU WILL NEED

- A small blue spell candle
- A small black spell candle
- Matches
- A small bell
- A skirt (At the very least, tie a few scarves around your waist.)

1. Place the blue candle to your left and the black candle to your right. (Make sure that you only attempt this spell where you have enough room to spin safely without knocking over the candles: fire isn't Oya's thing, and you want to be safe.)

2. Light the black candle first, saying, *"Mama Oya, Lady of Storms, help my creativity to flow. Blow away all that is holding me back. Blow, Lady of Storms, blow."*

3. Now, light the blue candle, saying, *"I am seeking creative inspiration in (fill in the blank: what project do you feel stuck on?). As Oya blows, my ideas flow."*

4. Ring the bell nine times. Now it's time to dance: lift your arms and begin to spin counterclockwise. Whirl until you are dizzy, visualizing Oya's whirling energy as you move.

5. Let the candles burn until they are gone: leave them somewhere that your cat isn't likely to find, and keep an eye on the flames to make sure that all is well. Now, go tackle that project!

SPELL TO CONNECT WITH YOUR ANCESTORS

In her role as spirit guide, Oya can pass on any messages that you have for those who came before.

YOU WILL NEED

- A piece of black paper (Construction paper is excellent.)
- A light-colored pencil

1. Sit down on the floor in a comfortable position. Close your eyes, and picture Oya: her skin is as black as ebony,

and her head is covered in braids. Rainbow-colored beads dangle from the end of each braid, and when she shakes her head, you can hear the beads clacking and laughing. Picture her wide smile and her deep brown eyes.

2. With your eyes closed, say, *"Mama Oya, I come to you with respect. I am the daughter of (your mother's name), and she is the daughter of (your maternal grandmother). We are proud women, we are strong women, and I seek a connection with those who have gone before."*

3. Open your eyes and start writing whatever is in your mind. Don't read what you've written, and try not to think: for now, just write. When you run out of things to write, gently fold the paper in half and then in half again. Place it beneath your pillow, and in the morning, when you are fresh, read what you wrote. Whatever is on the page is beautiful: it's your first step toward connecting with and honoring your ancestors.

SPELL TO PROMOTE POWER

We're not talking about physical power: use this spell to empower your mind and spirit.

YOU WILL NEED

- A black bead (any type)
- A cord twice as long as your wrist (Hemp works best for this.)

1. Think about the ways you are mentally and emotionally strong. Say them out loud: *"I am strong in mind and heart because____."* Your list can be as long or as short as is natural.

2. Thread the bead onto the cord, holding it at the center of the cord. Tie a knot beneath the bead.

3. Now, think about the ways you wish you could be stronger. Say them out loud: *"I seek strength in____."*

4. Tie the cord on top of the bead. Now, your bead should be stationary, held between the first two knots. Tie three more knots above the bead, and three more knots below the bead. You have eight knots. Make the ninth knot (sacred to Oya) as you tie the bracelet around your wrist. (It's okay to ask someone to help you tie it on, if you need to.)

5. Wear the bracelet as often as you like: every day, or simply on special occasions when you need as much strength as you can get.

CHAPTER 2

Making Love (and Lust) Last

Tears were streaming down my face. My two best friends looked on in stunned confusion.

"Did Matt do something?" One of my friends squeezed my hand as she asked that tough question, and I could practically see the calculations whirring behind her eyes, figuring out how to best cancel the plans of the afternoon if my answer were yes. Wordless, I shook my head, tears still un-stemmed.

"Are you having second thoughts?" Again, I shook my head. Although my answers had not explained the situation, both of these women breathed a sigh of relief. Whatever was wrong with me was not something which, they seemed to feel, would really matter in the grand scheme of my wedding day. They turned back to the preparatory tasks they had shouldered, pausing to bring me a sandwich and squeeze my shoulder, but they seemed unconcerned about my bizarre tears. Relieved somewhat, now that I had been faced with two of the more frightening questions to consider a few hours before vowing my life to another soul, I sat, sniffling as my tears subsided, trying to readjust my mood to fit the joy of the day.

Even now, I am still not sure why I spent the hours leading up to my wedding crying, but these two friends knew me well enough to cut straight to the heart of the matter with their questions. While I do not know what prompted the tears, I do know that I might never have stopped crying had it not been for these women. They held me up, boosted my spirits, and sang old doo-wop with me while I prepared to step out of single girlhood and into marriage.

Relationships are the foundation of our existence: we cannot survive without some contact with others. There are lovers and partners, friends and companions, and those to whom we are bound by blood. However, despite their importance, relationships are rarely easy. Sometimes, a little magical assistance is necessary to keep things running smoothly.

The spells contained in this chapter will not make anybody fall in love with you, nor will they suddenly make your relationship with your mother perfect. Rather, they will help you find your own footing in your relationships, giving you strength and confidence in your dealings with others. Aphrodite is a goddess who specializes in love, while Persephone has learned the hard way how to balance her partner and her mother. Mary, the mother of Christ, may not be a goddess in the traditional sense, but she is still an ideal figure to go to if your familial relationships are in danger. Hera will help you build a strong marriage with the right partner, and Parvati knows how to balance her lover and her child into a harmonious family. With their help and a little bit of magic, you will find that your relationships can be even better than you imagined.

Aphrodite

Titles: Lady of Cyprus, Well-Breasted One, Morning Star

Attributes: Water, Passion, Lust, Growth, Abundance

Colors: Pink, Red, Gold

Animals: Dove, Dolphin, Serpent

Culture of Origin: Pre-Greek/Hellenistic

You're probably already familiar with this shmexy goddess in one form or another. Aphrodite is one of those gals who transcends the bounds of time, probably because she's associated with one of our deepest urges: love. While there's a fair amount of lust in her stories as well, Aphrodite is the quintessential goddess of love.

Her birth is rather, erm, sticky. When Cronus (the Titanic precursor to the Olympians) battled with his father, the sky god Uranus, Cronus fought dirty. His sickle headed straight for daddy's privates, and when the bits fell from the sky, they landed in the sea. Out of the resulting foam, Aphrodite was born. She has a place in the Greek pantheon, but just like Athena, her origin story hints at a pre-existing goddess. Something about her endures, regardless of which culture is currently in power.

Unlike her Roman counterpart Venus, Aphrodite is known for her acts of revenge and lack of foresight. Remember the apple competition that Athena lost? Aphrodite won by promising to give Paris the most beautiful woman on earth. Did it matter that Helen was already married, and that her promise would start a disastrous war that would stretch for ten years? Not to Aphrodite: she'll promise anything as long as she ends up on top of the deal.

In an effort to keep this lusty goddess under control, Zeus handed her off to his son Hephaestus, but it wasn't the crippled blacksmith Aphrodite had her eye on. In true mythic soap opera style, the goddess had multiple affairs, never bothering to hide her actions. Her most famous affair was, get this, with poor Hephaestus's brother, Ares. Aphrodite had a score of children with the god of war, including her most famous child, Eros (although you probably know him as Cupid).

This is not a goddess known for her kindness. Aphrodite is powerful, make no mistake about that, but time and again, her stories tell us that she can be as fickle as infatuation, flitting from lover to lover on a never-ending quest to be deemed "the fairest of them all." This goddess has a certain amount of vanity, much like the fairy-tale queens immortalized by the Grimm brothers. As in those stories, Aphrodite can be a dangerous enemy. But she is also an incredible ally.

Whether they were mortals or gods, it seems like it was impossible for anyone to resist Aphrodite's charms. This goddess spread throughout the Greco-Roman empires, and she's still a popular figure to this day. But what can we learn from this magnificent, arrogant goddess?

Working with Aphrodite is like dancing over fire: potentially dangerous, but insanely powerful. If your love life needs a jolt, she's your girl. Whenever you feel the mundane world getting under your skin, let Aphrodite remind you that you, too, are a goddess. Just remember: she's the fairest of them all. Paris said so: don't even think about challenging her title.

SPELL TO SPICE UP YOUR NIGHTS

This isn't a spell you perform on your lover: this is a spell to help you reach your full sexy potential with or without assistance.

YOU WILL NEED

- A bathtub (Adding oils, salts, and bubbles is *always* okay with Aphrodite.)
- Candles (Optional: Any kind is okay.)
- Matches
- A red rose

1. First, fill the tub. Make sure the water is hot, and add any scents or bubbles that you want. If you aren't a bubble person, that's okay, too. Light the candles if you want to add to the ambience.

2. Make sure you won't be disturbed for awhile.

3. Before you get into the bath, pluck the petals from the rose, one by one. Drop them into the bath. As you do this, say, *"Aphrodite, goddess of love, infuse me with your vibrancy. Fill me with your fire. Let me never be unsatisfied."*

4. Once the rose petals are all floating in the water, get into the tub. Close your eyes and relax. Think about what makes you feel sexy. What turns you on? Allow your thoughts to wander, exploring fantasies or remembering times when you felt like you were on fire (in a good way, of course).

5. Leave the tub before the water starts to cool off. As you drain the water, say, *"I have the same essence as Aphrodite. Fire flows in my veins."* Don't worry about cleaning up now: take care of the petals tomorrow.

6. I'd recommend doing this before a hot date, or when you've been in a bit of a sex slump. Aphrodite loves to get your blood flowing and your heart racing!

SPELL FOR ENHANCED CONFIDENCE

It can be hard to find love when you are down in the dumps. Use this spell to get a boost of Aphrodite's infinite self-confidence, and strut your stuff.

YOU WILL NEED

- Some money to spend (maybe $20—in cash)
- Time
- A favorite place to shop

1. When was the last time you bought a power object? We can turn just about anything into a talisman or charm, but it's good to treat yourself when working with Aphrodite. Before you begin this spell, hold the cash that you

are going to spend. Say, *"Aphrodite, with this offering, I ask to share your confidence."*

2. Travel to your favorite store, and scout around for an unnecessary feel-good item. It can be a ring, a scarf, or a pair of skinny jeans, but here's the catch: it has to be something you can wear.

3. You'll know it when you see it: that thing that makes you smile wider, that you just have to have but feel like is impractical. That's what you're looking for.

4. Pay for the object with the cash you charged earlier. Don't take a bag: wear it out of the store (even if you have to stop in the restroom and change).

5. Whenever you feel your confidence slipping and you need a boost, put on your special object. Each time you wear it, remember to say, *"Thanks to Aphrodite, I am filled with light."*

SPELL FOR PASSION

Are you going on a first date or trying to rekindle the romance with your longtime sweetie? Use this spell to enhance your passionate connection.

YOU WILL NEED

- Brownie mix (from scratch is fine, too, if you have the time)
- Cayenne pepper

- Cinnamon
- Muffin pans

1. Set up shop in your kitchen. Before you start mixing the brownies, say, *"Aphrodite, bless this sweet treat with your magic."*

2. Prepare the brownies as directed. Add a pinch of cayenne pepper and a bit more cinnamon right before you are done with the preparation. Say, *"Fill this food with fire. Let our passion ignite tonight."* While you are stirring in the pepper and cinnamon, think about your special someone.

3. Spray the muffin cups with cooking spray, and fill each one halfway with brownie mix. Bake the brownie bites for the shortest time listed on the box, checking on them every ten minutes to make sure they don't burn. You want them cooked through, but not dry: use a toothpick in the center of the center brownie to test and see if they are cooked through.

4. When you serve these goodies to your love, make a fuss. Put them in a pretty container and drop them off at your lover's work, or bring them out as a surprise after a romantic meal. Wait for the passion to heat up.

Persephone

Titles: Lady of Flowers, Spring Maiden, Queen of the Dead

Attributes: Balance, Spring, Rebirth, Renewal, Pomegranates

Colors: Red, Black, White

Animals: Nocturnal Critters of the Air (Bats, Certain Predatory Birds)

Culture of Origin: Greco-Roman

Of all the messed up, misunderstood goddesses, Persephone is by far the most confused. Centuries of mythic structure—not to mention the Eleusinian Mysteries—tell us that this goddess was abducted, raped, and tricked into giving up the sunshine to return to the underworld each winter. But for anyone who's worked with Persephone, that's a hard version of events to swallow.

I find it much more empowering (and, frankly, much more appropriate) to consider Persephone not a passive victim, but a woman torn between her lover and her family. In choosing to marry the lord of the dead, she opted to move away from her fruitful mother Demeter, and in doing so, Persephone stepped out of the role of the devoted child and into her full woman-hood. Many modern writers have started to imagine what the story might be like if Persephone had knowingly taken a great risk rather than being kidnapped, but whichever version of the story resonates with you, Persephone is a figure of transition.

Her mother may never see her as an adult, but once she leaves home and is wed, she grows into her new self.

Now, that doesn't mean that the only way to differentiate yourself from that overbearing, well-meaning mother is to run off and get married. But regardless of how you separate yourself from your past, Persephone is a great goddess to turn to when you are ready to make the leap into the unknown.

Not only is this goddess adept at establishing her own identity and navigating the tricky waters of family relationships (she is, after all, married to her uncle), Persephone is a good lady to turn to for all matters of the heart. She's a pro at maintaining balance: she splits her time between her mother and her husband, and she also worked out a system to share hunky Adonis with Aphrodite, splitting his attentions the same way she splits her seasons. (Who knows what Hades had to say about all this.)

Persephone is strong. It takes a lot of inner fortitude to move beyond what's expected, especially when those preconceptions come from the ones we love. While Persephone isn't able to please everyone all of the time, she works hard to maintain balance between her family obligations and her heart. That's a lesson we could all use: it's hard to juggle our commitments to the ones we love. These spells will strengthen your ties to your loved ones, help you figure out which path to take, and show you the power of your choices.

Turn to this goddess for help finding your own voice, and seek her out when you are struggling to balance your relationships. Persephone may spend half her time in the underworld, but she's very in tune with the reality of relationships. It's hard to keep such a self-assured goddess in the dark!

SPELL FOR FINDING YOUR PATH

Persephone knows all about hard choices. Use this spell whenever you aren't sure which direction to go.

YOU WILL NEED

- A safe place to walk

1. I prefer to do this spell in early fall because I like to crunch through leaves while I'm thinking, but you can do this any time of year.

2. Set aside time to take a walk alone. Plan your route, and make sure you dress appropriately for the season. Before you leave, tell someone where you are going and how long you expect to be gone (a half hour is a good length of time for this spell).

3. Before you begin, say, *"What is my path?"*

4. Start walking. As you walk, carry on an inner dialogue. Go back to the question you asked before you began: What is your path? Where do you feel pulled right now? What are your obligations? What are your dreams? Are the two at war with each other, or can one help the other?

5. Walk briskly, letting your thoughts run in any direction that seems appropriate. If you get stuck, remember the goal of this spell, and ask yourself again, *"What is my path?"*

6. Walk for at least a half hour: when your mind slows down or an answer becomes obvious, you've probably been at it long enough. You may not receive your answer immediately, but it will come: trust the universe!

SPELL FOR FAMILY BALANCE

No matter who constitutes your family, sometimes it can be hard to please everyone. Use this spell to help you find balance in tricky situations.

YOU WILL NEED

- About six inches each of red, black, and white thread (I use embroidery floss, but yarn works, too.)

1. This spell is best done outside, or at least in a well-lit room. Take the three strands of thread. Tie a knot using all three threads at once, and try to position your knot as close to the center as possible.

2. Say, *"I am bound by ties of love."* Starting above the knot first, begin to braid the three threads. Tie off the end. Now, begin to braid the threads beneath the knot. Tie off the threads.

3. Put this charm in your kitchen (the junk drawer is an ideal place). Whenever you are feeling stretched or stressed about your family, take out the charm and look at it.

Repeat this spell every year as needed: right around Thanksgiving seems to be a good time, since that's usually when we need to remember not to kill our families.

SPELL FOR TOUGH CHOICES

Sometimes, you'll find yourself struggling to make a decision. Use this spell to clear your mind and move forward.

YOU WILL NEED

- A pomegranate
- A knife
- A bowl of cold water

1. Before you begin, say, *"Persephone, you stand by your choices. Help me to do the same."*

2. Slice the top off the pomegranate. You'll probably want to use a cutting board. Score the pomegranate five times (like a star) and set it into the bowl of cold water, open side down.

3. Think about the choice that you are facing. What are the options on the table? Which option frightens you? Which option entices you? Are the options pretty much equal?

4. After about five minutes, begin peeling the pomegranate. Drop the seeds into a bowl or small colander, and keep thinking about your choice as you work.

5. Eat one seed. Say, *"A choice must be made."*

6. Divide the rest of the seeds into piles based on the number of things you are choosing between. Do this one seed at a time (sort of like picking the petals off a daisy). For each seed, think about a positive thing that relates to that choice. You can even say these things out loud.

7. Start building the piles equally (one for choice A, one for choice B, and so on), but as you work, your gut will take over. One pile will grow larger than the others, and this will tell you your choice.

8. Leave the remaining seeds outside as an offering.

9. Eat the seeds from the chosen pile one at a time, savoring the good things about this choice.

Mary, Queen of Heaven

Titles: Queen of Heaven, Most Pure One, Mother of Christ, Our Lady, Lady of Sorrows

Attributes: Virginity, Motherhood, Patience, Suffering, Sorrow

Colors: Blue, White, Gold

Animal: Dove

Culture of Origin: Judeo-Christian

You're probably wondering what the dominant female figure in Christianity is doing in a book of goddess magic. Mary is an interesting figure: within the monotheistic context, she fulfills the necessary role of the divine feminine, acting as a goddess in all but name. Worried about what God the Father will say or do? Talk to Mother Mary. Praying for children? She understands. Seeking comfort in sorrow? Who else besides Mary knows how deeply suffering can cut?

In Christian myth, Mary was a simple young woman marked by God. She met an angel and was informed that she would bear a divine child. Did she freak out or get a big head? Nope. Mary went about her business quietly, confiding in her closest friends, including her confused fiancé Joseph. She even quietly bore the baby in a barn, without medical assistance, far from home. That's strength!

After the foretold birth, Mary and her family went on the run for years. They headed to Egypt, where the gods wore animal heads and the language was strange. There's no doubt that Mary was frightened: she was a young mother in a strange land, struggling to keep her precious child safe from those who threatened him. It must have been excruciating for her to let him grow up: she'd always known the way her son's myth would play out. But still she raised him with love and tenderness and sought to make a new life in Egypt for as long as was necessary. When the time finally came for her son to lay down his life, Mary didn't stop him. She stayed at the foot of the cross to keep him company, even though his pain must have crippled her.

Although the story of the sacrifice of the divine son isn't a new one, Mary's position has endured where many goddesses have faded. She's even absorbed one of the ancient titles given to goddesses in the Mediterranean: Queen of Heaven. Later amendments to her myth make her even more otherworldly: not only did she supposedly bear a child without sex, she herself is said to have been born from a similar divine union. And when Mary's life was at an end, angels descended from heaven and carried her, still living, into the sky. She never actually died: if that isn't a goddess, I don't know what is!

That's all well and good, but how does one work magic with Mother Mary? The faith structure that surrounds her frowns upon the occult, but that shouldn't stop you from reaching out to this nurturing figure, especially in times of family turmoil. Mary isn't judgmental, and at her core, she's a mother who only wants what's best for her family.

You might not be a mother, but we've all experienced family crises from time to time. When tempers start to flare, turn to Mary to get you through the disaster. She's also a good lady to talk to when you or your loved ones need emotional protection. Mary doesn't ask for much in return, but I like to light a candle for her whenever I find myself in a Christian church.

SPELL TO EASE TENSION

Sometimes, families get sick of one another. Use this spell to get past the rough spots.

YOU WILL NEED

- Olive oil
- A family recipe (Casseroles are especially good for this.)
- An excuse to gather your family together for a meal (maybe a holiday, if you are distant from your kin)

1. Assemble the ingredients you will need for the recipe. Make sure you have everything: it's never fun to stop in the middle of a kitchen project to search for the butter.

2. Say, *"Mary, Mother, bless this meal and the hands that will prepare it. Help me bring love to the table today."*

3. Dip your fingertips in the olive oil, and press your hands together in a prayer at your heart.

4. Start cooking. While you work, focus your thoughts on the things you love about your family. Maybe Uncle Joe always makes you laugh, and maybe your mom has a great sense of style. Don't think about the negativity that's prompted this spell: keep your thoughts positive.

5. Set the table. Make a production of it: place mats, napkins, tablecloth, the fine china, whatever is out of the norm for you. You want to soothe your family, after all: make them feel special.

6. Before the meal, say a quick blessing, like, *"We give thanks for this bounty, and for a reason to eat together."*

7. As you share this meal with your family, try to steer the conversation in a positive direction. Mary will take care of the rest!

SPELL FOR GRIEF

We will lose the ones we love, but we don't have to lose our will to keep loving.

YOU WILL NEED

- A blue spell candle
- Matches
- An hour of undisturbed time

1. Sit in a quiet, dark room with the unlit candle in front of you. Make sure you are in a comfortable position.

2. Say, *"Holy Mary, Lady of Sorrows, be with me in my grief."*

3. Light the candle.

4. Stay in the room until the candle goes out. You can talk to Mary, or to the person you are grieving for, or you can just sit in silence. There is no right way to grieve: listen to your heart, and follow your instincts.

5. When the candle has burned itself out, stretch and stand up slowly. Say, *"I am never alone in my grief."* Remember that: Mary is always there when you mourn.

SPELL FOR TRUST

Sometimes, we find it hard to recover from the wounds of the past. Seek Mary's help when you are having trouble trusting.

YOU WILL NEED

- A sheet of paper
- Something to write with
- An envelope
- A bowl of cool water (for the second phase of the spell)

1. Who is the person you are struggling to trust? Think of her clearly, and remember why you want to trust her. Think about why you are unable to trust her.

2. Write a letter to this person. Say anything, but it's especially powerful if you explain the reasons you are struggling with trust. Make sure you also include in the letter the fact that you *want* to trust this person again.

3. Seal the letter in the envelope. Put it somewhere safe and out of sight. Say, *"Mother Mary, may I find trust in my heart."*

4. Leave the envelope alone until things change with the specific person. Once you feel that you are beyond your trust hurdle, submerse the still-sealed envelope in a bowl of cool water. Let it soak: it should start to get pulpy.

5. Throw the soggy letter on your garden or compost heap, or, if you don't have either, put it out with the trash.

Hera

Titles: Queen of Heaven, Mother of the Gods, Lofty One, Cow-Eyed

Attributes: Marriage, Childbirth, Fidelity, Women's Rites

Colors: Gold, Purple

Animals: Peacock, Cow

Culture of Origin: Pre-Greek/Hellenistic

There's a lot more to Hera than the image of the perpetually jealous wife. This feisty goddess never shies away from conflict, even when she ends up on the losing side. It's likely that Hera, like Athena and Aphrodite, predates the Greek myths as an autonomous goddess, but it can be hard to separate her old self from her new self.

Hera is said to be the sister-wife of Zeus, and as such, she is the reigning queen of the Olympians. Although she's the goddess of marriage and fidelity, her own union started with deceit and stretched on for centuries of unhappiness. Zeus was already quite the player when he set his sights on Hera: perhaps he hoped to cement his claim to the throne of Olympus by tying himself to this powerful goddess. Hera was no fool: she laughed at his advances, content to keep her sovereignty for herself.

But "no" never stopped Zeus. He knew that Hera was compassionate, and so he hatched a plan. He shape-shifted, something he did a lot to catch his next romantic conquest, into a poor, bedraggled bird. When Hera caught sight of the little guy, she scooped him up and held him tenderly on her lap. Of course, this was the opportunity Zeus had been waiting for; he transformed back into his godly self, raped her, and then forced her to marry him. It's not a pretty story, but Hera is deeply committed to tradition, and the loss of her virginity meant one thing: as the goddess of marriage, she was shamed into her own union.

Don't let the story fool you: Hera may have been victimized once, but she never let Zeus have a moment's peace after that. She watched him carefully, and every time he sauntered off to seduce another mortal, Hera followed. It's in this role that most people remember her: the jealous woman, tormenting unsuspecting mortals and carrying a deep grudge toward her husband's heroic spawn. But every time Hera struck out in this manner, she was venting her rage toward her abusive husband.

She didn't punish every hero; in fact, she had a soft spot for those lusty young men who weren't the result of her husband's philandering. She championed Jason as he traveled

with the Argonauts, but when Jason broke his marriage vows, he lost Hera's support. For her, family and tradition trump all.

Hera is a great goddess to work with when you are seeking a committed relationship, but remember, she doesn't look kindly on infidelity or broken vows. Only work with Hera when you are sure you want to commit to your partner. If you haven't found the right partner yet, Hera can help you decide who will be the best match. Proceed with caution: there's nothing Hera hates more than flaky dishonesty. It's okay to turn to Hera for guidance, too: you don't have to know whom you want to spend your life with to work with her. She's great for finding your own inner queen and learning to face what comes.

SPELL FOR FINDING A MATCH

It's hard to be single, but if you're ready for lasting love, ask Hera to show you the way.

YOU WILL NEED

- A "gold" ring (A novelty ring is fine, unless you have a piece of fancy jewelry you want to use.)
- A long cord (Leather is best: it should be thin enough for the ring to slide easily on it.)

1. Hold the cord in your left hand and the ring in your right. Say, *"Golden Hera, Goddess of Marriage, I am looking for my match."*

2. Thread the ring onto the cord, and tie the cord around your neck. Say, *"I am ready to find someone loyal and true, and I am ready to be loyal and true."*

3. Repeat this spell daily as you search for your love. For added oomph, you can place the cord and ring under your pillow while you sleep.

SPELL FOR A HAPPY RELATIONSHIP

Even though Hera's marriage isn't great, she still wants you to have a wonderful relationship. Ask her for help!

YOU WILL NEED

- A picture of you and your partner
- An incense burner
- A stick of incense (Patchouli or rose is best.)
- Matches

1. Take the image of you and your partner. Think about your relationship. When did you meet? What are some of your favorite memories? When did your partner make you laugh so hard you almost cried? Focus on the joyous memories, regardless of how long you've been together.

2. Set the picture down beside the incense burner.

3. Say, *"Hera, I ask that you bless this relationship with bliss. May our happiness outweigh our trials."*

4. Light the incense.

5. Leave the picture beside the incense. The smoke will carry your intentions to Hera in the heavens.

6. Repeat this ritual as needed, especially if your relationship hits a rocky patch.

SPELL FOR A STRONG MARRIAGE

You can do this spell for yourself, or as a gift to a friend on the eve of her wedding. If you gift this spell, make sure you hand over the bag immediately.

YOU WILL NEED

- A small cotton bag with a drawstring
- Fennel seeds (1 tsp)
- Dried rosemary (1 tsp)
- Dried orange peel (1 tbsp)
- Cloves (1 tsp: Ground is fine.)
- Two gold rings (You can buy fake wedding bands at most craft stores.)

1. Open the drawstring bag. Say, *"Into this bag I add strength, protection, joy, and passion."*

2. Add the herbs one at a time. Start with the fennel seeds, followed by rosemary. Next, add the orange peel, and last, throw in the cloves.

3. Put the rings in the bag. Say, *"May this marriage be blissfully blessed. Hera, watch over this union."*

4. Pull the string tight. Give the bag a few shakes, to allow the herbs a chance to mix and mingle.

5. Say, *"Hera, please watch over (name) and (name). Bless this union."*

6. If you made the bag for yourself, keep it tucked in your underwear drawer. If you made it for a friend, give it to her on her wedding day, and tell her to put it in her underwear drawer.

7. Don't open the bag. Keep it as long as the relationship lasts, but if the marriage should end, burn the bag.

Parvati

Titles: Devoted One, Great Wife, Mother of Mountains, She-Who-Is-Pure

Attributes: Persistence, Sexuality, Partnership, Motherhood, Creative Power, Energy

Colors: White, Gold, Red, Orange

Animals: Lion, Tiger

Culture of Origin: India (Hindu)

When the Hindu god Shiva lost his beloved first wife, there was no one who could snap him out of his deep depression. But then Parvati showed up. She's actually the reincarnation of Shiva's first wife, but that didn't mean she had an easy road ahead of her. Born to a mortal family, she knew at an early age that she wanted nothing more than to please Shiva. But the god was so wrapped up in sadness that he didn't notice her. She decided to force him to see her.

Parvati worked hard to win Shiva's favor. She lived a blameless life, working with the poor in Shiva's name. She collected offerings and donations and delivered them to the god. Her own divine nature started to shine through, and finally, Shiva took notice of her. Their marriage was marked with intense sexual passion, and it is said that Parvati is the perfect complement to Shiva in all things. Parvati is revered as a powerful goddess in her own right. Her creative and protective powers are vast, and she's not just a devoted sex kitten: she's a fiercely loyal mother.

Parvati has two children, but her son, Ganesha, is her own creation. Shiva was not involved in Ganesha's birth; some say that Shiva forbid Parvati from having children, so that he could keep her all to himself, but others simply tell the tale that Shiva was away when Parvati conceived Ganesha. Either way, Ganesha is 100 percent Parvati's unique creation. She made his body out of red river mud, and told her son to guard her while she was in her bath. He agreed to do whatever she asked, and loyally watched over his goddess mother. But when Shiva came home and demanded admittance, Ganesha stopped him. Enraged, the god cut off the boy's head.

Only later, when Parvati saw the corpse of her child, did Shiva realize what he'd done. Parvati's rage knew no bounds, and all the gods struggled to appease her. They attached the head of an elephant to her son's body, breathing life back into him, but that wasn't enough. Parvati insisted that her son be deified and honored as a god by all people. The rest of the gods readily agreed: Parvati wasn't a passive force when she was angry, and they wanted their beloved goddess back.

Parvati is a mother and a wife, but she is also an example of single-minded determination. Whatever this goddess sets her mind on, she achieves. Seek her assistance when you are struggling to reach a seemingly unattainable goal, or when you want to catch the eye of a particular person. She can help you become more loyal in your love relationships, and she is also an excellent goddess to turn to when you find yourself torn between your lover and your child.

SPELL FOR DEDICATION

This spell can be applied for just about anything, but creative projects and lifestyle changes work best. If you feel your enthusiasm flagging, Parvati can help you get back on track.

YOU WILL NEED

- Scraps of paper (They should be large enough to write on: sticky notes work well.)
- Something to write with
- An offering bowl (Any bowl will do.)
- A yellow spell candle
- Matches

1. Say, *"Parvati, Devoted One, I ask your help. I want to dedicate my heart to (whatever it is). Show me the path."*

2. On the scraps of paper, write down words that describe the object of your dedication: is this a project, a way of life, a belief system? As you fill each scrap, place it in the offering bowl.

3. When you've filled all the paper (or run out of things to say), set the yellow spell candle carefully in the offering bowl. You may have to move the paper around to find a flat surface for the candle: just don't take the paper out of the bowl.

4. Light the candle and say, *"My intentions are set. From this day forward, I am dedicated to (whatever it is). With your help, Parvati, I will honor this choice."*

5. Snuff out the candle, but leave everything in the bowl.

6. If you feel your dedication flagging, light the candle again, repeating the statement in step 4.

SPELL TO BREAK A DEDICATION

Sometimes, a lack of dedication means you are unfocused, but other times, it means that you are trying to dedicate yourself to something or someone that may be harmful for you. If that's the case, this spell can help.

YOU WILL NEED

- Scraps of paper (If you completed the previous spell but now want to undo it, use the paper from that spell.)
- Something to write with
- A fire-safe bowl (Cast iron works great.)
- Matches
- Water
- Salt

1. What is the dedication you want to break? Why are you seeking to free yourself? Write down the reasons that this vow no longer serves you, either on fresh paper or on the back of the scraps from the previous spell.

2. Place the paper in a fire-safe container.

3. Say, *"Parvati, your dedication is astonishing. I want to follow in your footsteps, but I must un-swear myself from (the thing that you want to quit). This vow no longer serves me, but I do not break it lightly. I ask your blessing as I strive to honor my heart."*

4. Light a match and toss it into the container. Paper sometimes takes time to catch on fire, so it's okay if you need to use more than one match.

5. Once the paper is burning, say, *"Vows should not be made or broken lightly. Parvati, guide my steps and guard my heart."*

6. When the paper has been burned to ash, douse the container with water. Make sure everything is cool before you dispose of the ashes. Throw them away; don't put these ashes on your garden.

7. Clean the fireproof bowl with salt and water.

SPELL FOR SEXUAL COMPATIBILITY

Shiva and Parvati have a love life that's legendary. Want to add some of their magic to your relationship?

YOU WILL NEED

- A blank journal (Pick something that looks sexy to both you and your partner.)
- A willing partner

- Something to write with
- Time (This is an ongoing spell, not an instant jolt.)

1. Ask your partner if he/she would be willing to keep a sexual journal with you. If the answer is yes, proceed to step 2!

2. Hold the blank journal on your lap. (You can do steps 2 and 3 alone.) Say, *"Parvati, my love and I long for the bliss you have found with Shiva. Bless our union, and guide our attempts to please each other."*

3. Write down anything that you enjoy sexually. Feel free to write down unfulfilled fantasies, too.

4. Give the journal to your partner to complete step 3.

5. Swap the journal back and forth, reading what the other has written. Have a discussion: what can you do to meet each other's needs?

6. Keep the journal by your bed, and the next time your partner wants to get frisky, try to remember the things that you both wrote in the journal.

7. Return to the journal as often as needed: use this as a tool to facilitate communication. Sometimes, it can be hard to tell somebody what you want, but writing it down is much easier. The journal holds you both accountable, too: no more excuses!

8. Keep an open mind, and watch your relationship deepen.

CHAPTER 3

There's No Place Like Home

My husband bought a weed whacker this weekend. If I didn't know better, I might simply smile and say, "Ah, men and their gadgets," and leave it at that. Don't get me wrong: my husband loves gadgets and technology, but that's not why he bought this latest device. He purchased it as an artistic tool, much like a paintbrush or a calligraphy pen.

Yes, you heard me correctly. Weed whacking is an art form to my husband. The garden is his canvas. He spends hours drafting detailed sketches of bird's-eye views of what our piece of earth will look like when he's done trimming and planting and rearranging. But just the sketching is not enough: his creative soul demands the tangible, three-dimensional results of a rain garden and raised beds. His need to create is one that I understand.

Like my mother and grandmother, I enjoy baking. Whereas their specialty is cookies, I am most enthralled with bread making of late. I grew up with a bread machine, so handmade bread was not a craft I had much connection with. But now that I have claimed my own adulthood, I have discovered the joy and deep spiritual satisfaction of this process. Once a month, I set aside the hours needed to watch the dough rise, punch it down, let it rise again, and finally braid it into something beautiful.

When I bake, I not only surrender myself to the fire of creativity that lights every soul: I also consciously pay homage to the Goddess. My loaves of bread are three braided strands of dough, a tangible, edible reminder to me of the Trinity that I bow to. When I work to create food that will nourish my household, I enter into a meditative space, transforming the kitchen into a temple. This is one of the spells I will share with you in this chapter.

The goddesses detailed in this section are all ideal when you are working in your home to create sacred beauty and everyday magic. Brigid teaches homey creativity, while Hestia guards and blesses the hearth fire. Juno can be called on to protect the inhabitants of your home, and Bast will bring playful joy into your space. Changing Woman helps you remain flexible, reminding you that everything comes in its season. With their help, use these spells to create a home that is safe and filled with light.

Brigid

Titles: Foster Mother of Christ, White Lady, Triple
Goddess, Bright One

Attributes: Fire, Creativity, Smithcraft, Jewelry
Making, Baking, Dairy Products, Poetry

Colors: White, Red, Yellow

Animals: Sheep, Cattle

Culture of Origin: Irish/Celtic

Not to play favorites, but Brigid is one of the goddesses whom
I really feel a connection with. I discovered her early in my
quest for female divinity, and something about her fiery and
at the same time nurturing spirit really spoke to me. Probably
it's the poet in me: Brigid loves poets and their craft, and her
inspiration has fueled many a bard. She's also a classic example
of a triple goddess, embodying aspects of the maiden, mother,
and crone archetypes within herself. She's a three for one deal!
It's hard to talk about Brigid the goddess without acknowledg-
ing the role of Brigid the saint: her two identities
have become so closely linked that it's not always
clear where one ends and the other begins.

Brigid was the daughter of fairy, literally: her father, Dagda, is one of the great Fey gods of Ireland.
She was known for her way with the sacred cattle,
and that animal is still associated with her. Somewhere
along the way (perhaps in her guise as a saint), she de-
veloped a connection with sheep, particularly the mother ewes

and their first lambs, and many people still celebrate Brigid in early February. Some call the feast Candlemas, while others name it Imbolc, but in either case, it is the turning of the year from darkness to light: the first spring feast celebrates the lactation of the ewes and the firstborn lambs. Brigid reminds us that darkness always gives way to light, just as winter always steps aside for springtime. At this holiday, Brigid's maternal associations are strong. Some even say that Brigid served as wet nurse and foster mother to the Christ Child, rearing him on the mystical green isle and imparting to him all the wisdom of the druids.

Another story where the line between goddess and saint is blurred tells of Brigid's healing arts. Two lepers approached the well in Kildare, a spot so sacred to the goddess that even in the convent that replaced her temple, a sacred flame was tended by the acolytes well into the late Middle Ages. The men asked for Brigid's blessing, seeking to be healed from their horrible disease. She appeared before them, and, as goddesses are wont to do, she tested them. They would be cured of all illness, she said, if each man bathed the other in the waters of the sacred well. One leper completed the task without complaint, but the moment his companion was healed, he backed out of his part of the bargain. Now that he was healthy, he didn't want to touch the rotted skin of his friend. Brigid was, understandably, annoyed. She turned the man back into a leper and cured the one who had been willing to help his companion. Like many maternal goddesses, Brigid has a backbone of steel; this goddess isn't a friendly pushover.

Work with Brigid to infuse your daily life with creativity and warmth. Her fiery energy can turn even the most mundane chores into something magical, and she's also a great goddess to turn to when you need a nourishing boost. Use these spells to energize the mundane, and let Brigid help you find magic in every moment.

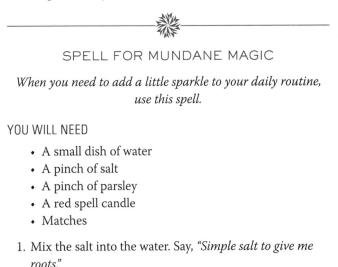

SPELL FOR MUNDANE MAGIC

When you need to add a little sparkle to your daily routine, use this spell.

YOU WILL NEED

- A small dish of water
- A pinch of salt
- A pinch of parsley
- A red spell candle
- Matches

1. Mix the salt into the water. Say, *"Simple salt to give me roots."*

2. Now, add the parsley. Say, *"Simple herb to bring fresh air."*

3. Light the red candle. Say, *"Brigid, by your flame and staff, infuse me with the joy of your craft."*

4. Stir the water clockwise with your finger. Drink it.

5. Extinguish the candle, saying, *"Simple things carry secret strength. There is magic in this moment."*

6. Save the candle: you can reuse it the next time you do this spell.

SPELL TO SPARK CREATIVITY

Use this spell whenever you have a creative project that needs a boost, or if you just want to change your daily routine.

YOU WILL NEED

- A small gray stone (Take it from your driveway or find it near your home.)
- A match

1. Sit outside or near a window for this spell.

2. Hold the stone in your nondominant hand, and the match in your dominant. (If you're left-handed, the match will be in your left hand, and vice versa.)

3. Close your eyes and listen to the sounds around you.

4. Breathe evenly. Take a deep breath, hold it for three seconds, and then exhale.

5. Repeat this focused breathing nine times.

6. With your eyes still closed, say, *"Let me carry this spark from day to day. Fill me with your flame, mighty Brigid."*

7. Strike the match against the stone as you open your eyes.

8. Keep the stone with you in your pocket, or leave it in the room where you want to be inspired.

SPELL FOR COMFORT

When you need the support of a hug, call on Brigid's maternal aspect to shelter you.

YOU WILL NEED

- A bread recipe (One that uses yeast and requires time to rise is necessary.)
- A few hours of quiet time
- Honey

1. Assemble your ingredients, and prepare the bread as the recipe instructs. I like to use an easy French bread recipe: most cookbooks have a few to choose from. Whichever you pick, don't make it too hard on yourself, especially if you've never made bread before. Essentially, all you need is flour, water, yeast, salt, and sugar.

2. As you mix the ingredients together, say, *"Goddess Brigid, Mother, guide my hand and hold me with your strong embrace."*

3. Let the dough rise as directed. If the recipe instructs you to knead it or punch it down, each time you do, say, *"Bless this bread, Brigid."*

4. When it's time to bake the bread, separate the dough into three equal-sized balls. Roll each ball out into a long dough snake.

5. Braid the braid. Starting in the middle of the three strands, place the left strand under the center. Now fold the right strand under the new center, and so on until the end of the loaf. Pinch the end together, and repeat the process with the other half of the bread.

6. Slice the braid with a knife (I slice along each exposed piece of the braid: this will allow the air to escape in the oven.)

7. Bake the bread as instructed.

8. When the bread comes out of the oven, break off a chunk with your hands. Eat it while it is still warm, but cool enough to handle. Dip the chunk in honey. Say, *"I ingest your warmth. Bring me comfort."*

9. Share the bread with your loved ones: Brigid Braids are best eaten within two days of baking. Don't forget to throw a piece outside for the goddess (and the birds).

Hestia

Titles: Keeper of the Flame, Hearth Woman, Mistress of the Home, Guardian of Mount Olympus

Attributes: Contained Fire, Creativity, Protection, Family, Hearth and Home

Colors: Black, Brown, Rust, White, Gold

Animals: Wren, Sparrow, Sow

Culture of Origin: Greco-Roman

Hestia is another homey goddess you might want to get to know. Although she's one of the original Olympians, this daughter of the old Titan Cronus didn't cling to fame the way her siblings did. When brassy, bold, Dionysus appeared on Olympus, Hestia gracefully stepped aside, leaving her throne open for the new god of wine and resurrection. She took her place beside the sacred hearth of the gods, tending the fire and listening to those around her. In time, the other Olympians seem to have forgotten her, but Hestia's quiet presence infused the sacred mountain with protection and the wonderful sense that there's no place like home.

When her dear old dad, Cronus, was swallowing his children (don't ask), Hestia was the firstborn, and so the first to meet the nasty, cannibalistic fate. Being divine, she didn't die, and when her youngest brother, Zeus, finally freed his siblings, Hestia was the last to be reborn. She holds a unique role: that of both the eldest sister and the youngest child of the divine family. Perhaps because she doesn't fit into a clear birth order, Hestia is a mutable goddess. She is often depicted as a crone, but she can take the maiden form, as well. Despite her brother's urging, Hestia refused all offers of marriage, choosing instead to tend the fire on Olympus in a state of perpetual virginity. She's another example of a multifaceted goddess, merging the roles of maiden and crone into one seamless whole.

As with Brigid, people honored Hestia with flame: the hearth was the literal heart of the home in ancient Greece,  and families gave the first morsels of their harvests and meals to Hestia to ensure her continued protection and blessing. Whenever a new city was founded in the Greek empire, sacred fire would be brought from Delphi, considered to be Hestia's home temple, to consecrate the space. Despite the fact that she doesn't show up much in myth, Hestia was a vital part of daily life to both the Greeks and the godly Olympians. You can't have a home without a hearth!

Working magic with Hestia is a simple matter: this isn't a goddess who favors a lot of loud, ceremonial gestures. When you are seeking protection for your home, or when you want to create sacred space out of a formerly mundane room, Hestia's your gal. Use the spells in this section to tap into the more nurturing side of fire: Hestia reminds us that fire can be soothing as it offers protection and nourishment to a household. Let her show you the softer side of fire magic.

SPELL FOR SACRED SPACE

Use this spell to boost any room from mundane to magical. I especially like to use this in my bedroom.

YOU WILL NEED

- Rosemary (a whole sprig, preferably fresh)
- A yellow flower (I like mums.)
- A twig (Find this on the ground near your home.)
- A piece of white ribbon or thread

1. Assemble the rosemary, flower, and twig in front of you. Arrange them in a bundle, with the stems aligned.

2. Take the white ribbon and slide it beneath the bundle. Say, *"Hestia, hearth keeper, help me make (the name or location of the space) sacred."*

3. Cross the two ends of the ribbon in the front of the bundle. Turn it over, and cross the two ends again. Repeat this step until you have just enough ribbon left to tie a knot.

4. Before you tie the knot, say, *"By the power of your sacred flame, I carry magic in your name."*

5. Tie the ribbon in a strong knot.

6. Hang the bundle on the south-facing wall of the room you want to sanctify. The bundle will dry, but that's okay. Leave it up, and look at it whenever you go into that room. Know that Hestia is keeping watch.

7. Repeat this spell once a year to recharge the same space, or every time you move.

SPELL FOR SAFETY

Use this spell to protect your home and those inside it from outside harm.

YOU WILL NEED

- A large white pillar candle
- Matches
- A small black stone (Hematite is my favorite.)

1. Hold the candle with both of your hands. Think about what it means to be safe.

2. Say, *"Safe and sound, may this space be safe and sound."*

3. Light the candle.

4. While it burns, think about the word *home*. What does this word mean to you? What memories are associated

with the idea of home? Let your thoughts take you wherever they will.

5. Next, think about safety: How do you feel safe? What makes you feel unsafe? What do you need to feel safer?

6. When the candle has burned enough to create a bowl of liquid wax, hold the black stone cupped in your palms.

7. Say, *"Hestia, bless my hearth and home. Shelter me and mine from harm, and give us shelter from the storm."*

8. Kiss the stone and drop it into the wax at the top of the candle. Be careful not to drop it too near the wick, or your candle will be extinguished. Leave the stone there: it's now a part of your hearth flame.

9. Blow out the candle. Light it once a month at the dark moon, repeating step 7 each time you do so.

SPELL FOR PEACE

Inner peace can be elusive, but use this spell whenever you are feeling wound up or distraught. Hestia can teach you a thing or two about being the calm within the storm.

YOU WILL NEED
- A small dish (preferably something pretty)
- A small white spell candle
- Matches

- Olives (I like to get the ones stuffed with garlic, but that's just because I like to ward off vampires . . . or maybe I just like Italian food.)

1. Set the dish in front of you, and sit in a comfortable position on the ground.

2. Place the candle in the dish, and surround it with olives (which may help hold it steady).

3. Light the candle, saying, *"Hestia, I share this time with you in hopes that you will share your peace and tranquility with me."*

4. Eat the olives slowly, one at a time. (If you don't like olives, you can just offer them all to Hestia.)

5. As you eat each olive, think about one aspect of your life that feels frantic or forced.

6. Talk to Hestia as you eat. Tell her your troubles, and listen to the sound of the candle flame burning in front of you.

7. When you are done, extinguish the candle by licking your fingers and pinching the wick.

8. Say, *"Hestia, thank you for sitting with me in stillness. May your peace and calm infuse my life."*

9. Leave at least one olive in the dish with the candle: I like to set mine outside on the porch for a squirrel to find.

10. Repeat this spell whenever you are feeling off-kilter.

$\mathcal{J}uno$

Titles: Goddess of Women, Mother of Rome,
Protector of the Legions, Guardian of the City

Attributes: Marriage, Motherhood, Female Coming
of Age, Protection, Security, Logic, Strength

Color: White

Animal: Goat

Culture of Origin: Latium/Roman

Although your social studies teacher might have said otherwise, Juno is not the same goddess as Hera. They share many attributes, and Juno absorbed some of Hera's mythology, but Juno existed in Italy as a distinctly separate goddess before the rise of Rome. It's hard to parse out the old Juno from the Hellenized one, but we can try.

To the Latins, the people who lived in southern Italy before the founding of Rome, Juno was literally within each woman. They believed that every woman had her Juno, her inherent femininity, just as each man had his Genius. As an archetypal spirit, Juno was so prevalent that when Aeneas and his invaders showed up, they absorbed the idea of Juno and turned her into the reigning female deity of the new culture. Roman culture was actually a motley assortment of myths and treasures from multiple people. The new Romans weren't picky about whom they borrowed from, and this trend continued throughout the rise and fall of the

Roman empire; other than Christianity and Judaism, most faiths were tolerated across the empire, and the conquering Romans didn't have a problem with absorbing gods and goddesses along the way.

As the wife of Jupiter and the figurehead for loyal marriage, Juno does not exhibit the same level of pettiness as is seen in Hera's stories. Rather, Juno is a reigning monarch in her own right: what does it matter if her husband is unfaithful when she has the loyalty of the entire Roman army? Rome took its military might seriously, and those well-trained men never marched off to conquer anybody without first praying to and sacrificing to Juno: you just don't leave home without asking for Ma's blessing.

Aside from her role as legionary mother, Juno was also one of the famous Capitoline Triad—the ruling body of all Roman affairs. Joined by Minerva and Jupiter, Juno was one of three deities whom Romans were required to worship. Most cities in the empire also had their own temples to the Capitoline Triad constructed. Juno was certainly not mocked as a jealous wife the way Hera was! Weakness and fiery passion weren't respected character traits in Rome, and no one would accuse Juno of either: this lady keeps a cool head and a calm heart, regardless of the circumstance.

Juno's protective qualities can be applied to your own life. It is said that she warned the citizens of Rome whenever disaster threatened, and you can use the spells in this section to create just such an alarm system for your own home. Turn to Juno when you need clarity and strength, and also seek her aid with any feminine problems, especially those related to your menstrual cycle. It may seem silly to ask such a powerful goddess for help with your cramps, but if anyone understands what it's like, Juno does.

SPELL FOR HOME PROTECTION

Use this spell whenever your home feels threatened, but remember, magic is no replacement for a strong lock and an alarm system.

YOU WILL NEED

- A bowl of salt
- Your house key
- A half-full glass of water

1. Set the bowl of salt in front of you. Have the key and the water on hand, as well.

2. Bury the key in the salt, saying, *"Juno, bless this space and make it safe. With your strength, my home is safe."*

3. Leave the key in the salt until you are ready to leave your house.

4. Now, pour the salt (key and all) into the water.

5. Take the salty water outside, and lock the door as you get ready to leave. Say, *"With your blessing, Mother of Rome, I ask defense upon my home."*

6. Pour the salt water out in front of your door. If you have multiple entry points, take a few minutes to walk around the house, sprinkling the water in front of each door.

7. Put your key back on your key ring, and proceed as usual with your day.

SPELL TO EASE CRAMPS

Sometimes, you just need a little magic to get through that time of the month.

YOU WILL NEED
- Milk (I use soy milk.)
- Your favorite (microwave-safe) mug
- A stirring implement
- Cinnamon
- Honey
- Vanilla

1. First, pour your milk into your favorite mug.

2. Heat the milk: about a minute and a half works in my microwave.

3. Stirring counterclockwise, add cinnamon, honey, and vanilla: a little goes a long way.

4. Sit in a quiet, dark place. Wrap up in a blanket or a sweater: get as cozy as you can.

5. Before you drink the concoction, say, *"Juno, Goddess of Women, help me ease the pain of womanhood."*

6. Sip the milk slowly. As you do, think about all the things that you enjoy about being a woman.

7. Before you drain the cup, say, *"Juno, help me bear this burden with pride."*

8. Finish your milk. Repeat as often as necessary.

SPELL FOR RESPECT

Use this spell whenever you feel like the world isn't taking you seriously. Juno understands.

YOU WILL NEED

- A mirror
- A hairbrush

1. Stand in front of a mirror. Study your reflection.

2. Say, *"I am bold and strong. I am* (your name), *and Juno rests within me."*

3. Touch the hairbrush to your chest, your lips, and your forehead. Watch yourself in the mirror.

4. Begin to brush your hair slowly. With each stroke, say, *"Juno within, Juno without."*

5. When you are done, set the hairbrush down. Look at yourself in the mirror. Say, *"I carry the power of Juno with me. I deserve respect, and I will continue to earn it."*

6. Repeat as often as needed. I find this especially good right before bed on nights before job interviews or other major events.

Bast

Titles: Eye of Ra, Mother of Cats, Lady of Joy, Little Lioness

Attributes: Protection, Pleasure, Solar Energy, Maternal Concerns, Household Guardian

Colors: Orange, Black

Animals: Domestic Cat, Lioness

Culture of Origin: Egypt

Don't be fooled by her cute little kitty face; Bast has fangs and claws, and this Egyptian goddess knows how to use them. Although more recent images and myths portray this goddess with the head of a house cat, in her earliest worship, she took the form of a lioness. When Sekhmet (discussed in chapter 1) grew in popularity, Bast's worship shifted to make room for another feline goddess, and Bast was gradually portrayed as a small cat, while Sekhmet was the fierce lioness. But size isn't everything, and Bast was one of the most popular goddesses in ancient Egypt, with her presence spanning dynasties.

Like Sekhmet, Bast bears the title "Eye of Ra." Many goddesses in the Egyptian pantheon share this name, which marks them as a powerful protector, one who is trusted to preserve not only the power of the sun, but the sacred natural order of the universe. It's no wonder Bast shares the title with others: that's a lot of responsibility for anyone, even a goddess!

In one tale, Bast is the right-hand man, er, cat, of the sun god Ra. It is only through her fierce attention and feline hunting prowess that Ra survived his nightly passage through the Duat, the underworld, to be reborn each morning at dawn. Bast is a mighty protector, and anyone who's ever watched a mama cat with her kittens will understand the strength of Bast's feline portrayal.

Bast isn't just about protection. Like any cat, she really knows how to have fun. Often paired with the house god Bes, Bast was celebrated with drunken revelry every year. The center of her worship, Bubastis, became a bustling, pulsing party for days and nights on end. This adults-only celebration was so popular in the ancient world that the historian Herodotus recorded it in great detail. (He probably partied, too: his descriptions are too exuberant for someone who just stood back watching.) This festival drew thousands of pilgrims, all intent on honoring the goddess by cutting loose and having a good time. Who wouldn't want an excuse to party around the clock, especially when such a party meant that you'd be blessed by this feisty goddess?

When you need a burst of playful energy, turn to Bast. She can inject any situation with joy and revelry, and she's also an ideal goddess to work with when you want your home to be a safe, welcoming place. Before throwing a party or going out for a night on the town, try the spells in this section. And if you have a house cat, remember that being good to her is a way to honor Bast!

SPELL FOR A GREAT PARTY

Want your next soirée to sparkle? Let Bast help you!

YOU WILL NEED

- Sangria (for summer parties)
- Oranges (for summer)
- A rich red wine (for winter)
- Cinnamon (for winter)
- A slow cooker (for winter)
- A large pitcher (I prefer plastic.)
- A pack of plastic cups (Red is not only classic, it makes Bast happy!)

1. Assemble your materials. If it's winter, you'll be heating the wine in the slow cooker, so you'll need to start about five hours before the party. If it's summer, you can do this an hour before guests arrive.

2. Pour the wine (warm or cold) into the pitcher. Say, *"Bast, with your help, this party will be the best yet."*

3. Add slices of orange to the sangria, or sprinkle cinnamon into the hot red wine. Say, *"Bless those who gather here, and fill us with your joyous warmth."*

4. Hold the unopened package of cups. Visualize your party: think about who will be there, what they will talk about, and how much fun everyone will have. Open the cups, and set them on your table or counter beside the charmed wine.

5. Once your guests arrive, let them serve the wine for themselves. Laughter and good feelings won't be far behind!

6. If you have any wine left over after the party, save it: don't drink Bast's wine alone. Have dinner with a friend soon after the party, and use up the rest of the wine. Or pour it outside as an offering.

SPELL FOR A HAPPY HOME

Whether you're in an apartment or a mansion, this spell will help make your home sparkle.

YOU WILL NEED

- 1 part white vinegar
- A spray bottle (If you have a cat, use a *different* bottle than your punishment bottle. Otherwise, Bast will be a bit annoyed.)

- 4 parts water
- Essential oil: lemon

1. Pour the vinegar into the spray bottle. Say, *"Vinegar clears away fear."*

2. Now add the water to the bottle. Say, *"Water clears away grime."*

3. Add four drops of lemon oil to the spray bottle. Say, *"Citrus fruit brings joy."*

4. Screw the cap on and give the bottle a good shake.

5. Walking clockwise around your home, spritz the mixture into the air. I also like to spray it on windows and mirrors (you can wipe them down an hour or two after the spell, to give the energy a chance to start working).

6. As you spray, say, *"Bast brings joy. May this home be happy. Safe from harm and filled with joy."*

7. Repeat this spell whenever you need a pick-me-up. You can reuse the same mixture until it runs out. Try to make a fresh batch at least once a year.

SPELL FOR SAFE FUN

Whether you're going out or staying in, you want your revelry to be safe and harmless. Ask Bast to watch over you!

YOU WILL NEED

- A piece of red thread long enough to tie around your wrist (Embroidery floss is best.)

1. After you shower, hold the red thread and say, *"Bast, watch over me. Keep me from harm while I play. Let my revels be safe, I do not want to be sorry."*

2. Tie the thread around your wrist. (You may end up using your teeth to get a knot, but that's okay.)

3. Get ready as you usually would. You can snip the loose ends of the thread or cover it with a bracelet. Whatever works for you!

4. Before you head off to wherever you're going, say, *"Bast keeps me safe. I know my limits."* Repeat this four times.

5. Have fun, remember to tell someone where you're going, and trust your instincts: listen to your gut if something feels strange or unsafe.

Changing Woman

Titles: Painted Woman, Eternal One, Renewed One, Earth Mother, Mother of All

Attributes: Renewal, Acceptance, Life Cycles, Womanhood, Transition

Colors: Rainbow, Green, Gold, Brown

Animals: All Mammals

Culture of Origin: Native American

This elusive goddess may originate in Apache myths, or she may come from the Navajo. Wherever she walks, however, it's easy to see how adaptable she is. Changing Woman is both the earth beneath our feet and the manifestation of the seasons of each year. She passes through youth to maturity, but death does not wait for Changing Woman. When she's reached her crone stage, this goddess simply walks into the east until she meets her younger self. When her old self and her young self meet, the two merge, leaving Changing Woman renewed and invigorated. She walks home, suddenly young, and starts her journey all over again. (What a great antiaging cream that would be: quick, somebody, figure out a way to bottle this!)

Like so many earthy goddesses, Changing Woman is a mother to all creatures on the earth. The earth is both her home and her body, and she understands the importance of caring for both aspects. Through her frequent renewal, she becomes better prepared to deal with the challenges that her children bring to her.

Some myths credit her with the creation of humanity, while others say that her body forms the very earth beneath our feet. She was sheltered by a rainbow when she was a child, and despite the changes she has endured over the centuries, this goddess is a constant optimist. There's always the possibility of renewal: if you walk far enough into your past, you will find the strength to create your future.

She's especially fond of young girls and women, and Changing Woman is always on hand to ease the life transitions women go through. When you got your first period, she rejoiced. When your heart broke for the fourth time, she sheltered you and wept for you. When you left home to create your own identity, Changing Woman was cheering in the stands, watching with interest to see what you would do with your new life.

Changing Woman is great to work with when you're feeling a bit nostalgic. She can help you appreciate where you were and how far you've come. She's also an excellent goddess to talk to during times of transition: through her example, we learn that change isn't something to be feared. With Changing Woman by your side, it's easy to remember that change is just another piece of the life cycle. Changing Woman will also serve as a reminder that no matter how far we walk from our pasts, eventually, we'll have to face what we've left behind. Sometimes, that can be a painful confrontation, but it doesn't need to be. Call on Changing Woman to help you accept all the facets of your life; past, present, and future are all one to her.

SPELL FOR FOND MEMORIES

Have you been thinking about the past lately? Celebrate your nostalgia with Changing Woman.

YOU WILL NEED

- Photographs from your past (Pick the ones that make you smile.)
- Scrapbook paper (Check the dollar store: you'll be amazed what you can find!)
- A small scrapbook album
- Scissors
- An acid-free glue stick
- A pen in your favorite color
- Stickers, fabric, ribbons (optional)

1. Assemble your craft supplies. Be prepared to spend a few hours at this: this is an ongoing spell.

2. Say, *"Changing Woman, help me to remember the past with joy."*

3. Look through the photographs. Pick one to start with: it doesn't have to be in chronological order. Just pick the one you are most drawn to.

4. Select a sheet of scrapbook paper. On the back, write down everything you remember about the photo you have chosen.

5. Using the glue stick, affix the picture to the front of the scrapbook paper however you want. Cut it in a shape, make a border for it, or decorate the page with ribbons. It's up to you.

6. Repeat steps 3–5 with each photograph. You can have more than one picture on a page, but make sure that you write at least one sentence about every picture on the back of the page it ends up on.

7. When you are done (or ready to take a break from this project), say, *"Changing Woman, Mother of All, thank you for walking with me through these memories. I am filled with joy."*

8. Repeat this spell whenever you are feeling a little nostalgic. When you've completed one album, you can always move on to another! Bonus: the albums make beautiful keepsakes, and they could be given as gifts to cherished loved ones if you choose. Keeping them is fine too; after all, they're filled with your memories!

SPELL FOR TRANSITION

Whenever you are facing a major transition in your life, let Changing Woman help you through it.

YOU WILL NEED
- A hot bath
- A handful of Epsom or bath salts

1. Fill the tub with hot water.

2. Lower yourself into the tub. Say, *"Everything changes."*

3. Cup the salts in your hands. Slowly spread your fingers, letting the salt crystals fall into the water.

4. With some salt still left on your hands, begin scrubbing your body. Start with your feet, and work your way up to your head. As you scrub, think about the things that are changing. What is the transition you are going through? How do you feel about this change? Don't judge your thoughts: it's okay to feel however you happen to feel.

5. Dip your hands into the water, and scoop up a handful. Lift it over your head and say, *"I am ready for this change."* Let the water trickle down your face.

6. When you are ready to get out of the tub, drain the water and rinse out any salt residue.

7. Go forward toward your transition. You are ready to face it.

SPELL FOR FLUID SPACE

Use this spell to create a safe space in your home where you are open to change. Changing Woman knows what you need!

YOU WILL NEED

- A prism or other clear crystal that has a hole in it for hanging (Bead stores are a good place to look.)
- Fishing line or clear jewelry thread
- A small suction cup

1. First, figure out which window in your house faces south or west (southwest is fine, too).

2. Look at where you want to hang the prism in this window, and cut the fishing line so that it's twice as long as you want it to be. Mine hangs down about a foot and a half, so my thread is three feet.

3. Say, *"Changing Woman, shine your light into my home. Let this be a place of fluid movement. No more will this be a stagnant place. Bring your motion into my space."*

4. Thread the prism and tie a tight double knot in the fishing line.

5. Affix the suction cup to the glass of your chosen window.

6. Hang the prism. Say, *"Changing, dancing, dreaming, living, laughing. Fill this home with your rainbow light."*

7. Every time you see the rainbows on your wall, remember Changing Woman: she's watching over your space, keeping you safe and receptive to change.

CHAPTER 4

When in Rome (or London, or Tokyo . . .)

When I turned twenty, I left the country alone for the first time. Sure, I'd been to Canada numerous times, but always with a friend or family member in tow. But that year, I booked a plane ticket and headed to China. One of the advantages of having really cool friends was that one of my longtime pals was teaching English in China, and he had always said that if I could afford a plane ticket, he'd show me around. So I guess I wasn't really alone, but I wouldn't meet up with him until after two flights: one from Chicago to Beijing, and the next from Beijing to the coastal city of Qingdao.

Since I'd never really traveled on my own, I didn't have a lot of methods or precautions in place. I hadn't yet learned to be anal about booking reservations (although that would be one lesson this trip would teach me), and I didn't even check with my friend before I bought the plane ticket. There was a holiday flight sale which looked like a good deal, so I bought a ticket for two weeks in the spring. Luckily, when I did call my friend, his spring break lined up with one of those weeks; we would be able to do some sightseeing together.

As the trip crept closer, I had so much fun buying adventurous clothes. For the first time in my life, I set foot in the sporting goods store on a mission to find clothes that would allow me to feel brave and backpacker-y. I wasn't taking a backpack, but that's beside the point. All my life, I'd dreamed of adventuring around the globe, and now I was finally getting the chance.

Even though I planned my wardrobe with care, I didn't really pay attention to the particulars of the trip. My friend told me there was no reason to book my connecting flight from Beijing to Qingdao ahead of time, so I didn't. But when I landed in Beijing Capital International Airport, I discovered something my friend had forgotten to mention: it was Chinese Labor Day, and the entire country was traveling. One more thing I hadn't been prepared for: nobody in the airport seemed to understand English.

After waiting in line at three ticket counters and not being able to make myself understood, I was on the verge of collapse. Luckily for me, a young woman who had been on my plane from Chicago spotted me. She left her luggage with her father (who had been waiting months to see her) and pushed her way to a fourth ticket counter. After a rapid fire exchange, she turned to me with a frown.

"There aren't any flights to Qingdao today. You can fly out tomorrow night at eleven."

I stared at her, confused. "But I have to get there today."

She shrugged. "You could try standby, but it probably won't work."

She embraced me before she left and wished me luck, and after I went into the bathroom and had a good cry, I resolved to handle the situation. Eventually, I made it to Qingdao after a day of waiting in the airport and a strange night spent at an expensive hotel, but the whole trip was colored by the panic I had felt when I landed in Beijing. Even though it was a once-in-a-lifetime experience, and even though the sites and people I encountered there were amazing, what the trip really taught me was that I am not a fly-by-the-seat-of-my-pants backpacking type. I still love to travel, but I like to have a plan; hotels booked well in advance, transportation confirmed before landing, and a schedule to stick to. The trip could have made me curl up into a little ball and refuse to travel again, but it didn't. Instead, the mistakes I made on my first expedition abroad taught me to form my own travel rules and to follow them.

The world is vast, and sometimes, it can be frightening. But there's so much beauty to experience: I don't want to be afraid to leave my comfort zone. The spells in this section will help you push your boundaries and find protection in unlikely places. Kali is a great goddess to work with when you need help breaking out of the norm, and Isis offers protection to all who seek it. Hecate travels through the realms with ease, and working with her can help you with your own transitions. Artemis will always protect women, and Gaia is the very earth beneath our globe-trotting feet. Use these spells when you are feeling unsure of yourself, and trust that the goddesses in this section will never let you stagnate.

Kali

Titles: Kali-Ma, The Destroyer, The Black One, Black Mother of Time

Attributes: Change, Destruction, Old Giving Way to New, Time, Protection, Freedom, Cemeteries

Colors: Black, Red

Animals: Snake, Tiger

Culture of Origin: India (Hindu)

This frightening goddess is one of the most powerful and beloved in the Hindu tradition, but Kali can sometimes be a bit overwhelming. In fact, she's always overwhelmed me: I tend to focus on her scarier aspects, but there's more to Kali than meets the eye. Kali is complex and impossible to know in one setting, but I'll do my best to give you an overview of this complicated Hindu goddess. Usually depicted with the heads of her victims dangling from her waist, Kali is the embodiment of protective, transformative energy. Only work with her if you are absolutely certain you are ready for a change!

In her creation myth, Kali is born to defend the gods in their darkest hour. After battling a regenerating demon, the goddess Durga is at her breaking point. From her despair (or her migraine), Kali is born, leaping onto the field of battle with a bloodlust that quickly makes short work of the demon and his minions.

In the wake of battle, Kali began to dance. The other gods watched, first in awe and then in terror, as her violent dance claimed not only the lives of the demons, but anything that landed underfoot. It was only when Kali's consort fell beneath her feet that she slowed her destructive gyrations. Luckily for Kali, the Hindu deities are adept at reincarnating themselves, so she didn't have to live with the guilt over slaying her lover forever.

Despite her fierce stories, Kali is a deeply beloved goddess. The poet and mystic Ramakrishna wrote of his deep and complicated relationship with Kali, comparing her to both a passionate lover and a fiercely loyal mother. At the core of her story, Kali personifies passion. Whether in the heat of battle or in the throes of sex (she's a favorite tantric figure, by the by), Kali never does anything halfway. Her fierce determination and unwavering bravery are both things that many modern girls wish for as we head out into the unknown.

When doing magic with Kali, it's a good idea to have some security measures in place. Even if you never cast a circle, I'd recommend doing so before attempting any of these spells. Also, be very specific in your requests to Kali; don't think you can outsmart any goddess—but especially not this one. And always remember Kali doesn't really have an off switch. If you ask her for help, be prepared to get out of her way and let her dance her transformative dance.

SPELL FOR MAJOR LIFE CHANGES

If you are going through major life changes, use this spell to gain clarity and strength.

YOU WILL NEED

- Your favorite blend of incense (Sandalwood is always good.)
- An incense burner
- Matches
- Red, black, and yellow thread, twice as long as your wrist (Ribbon or yarn is fine, too.)

1. Light the incense. Say, *"Mama Kali, help me be strong during this time of change."*

2. Tie the three threads together at one end.

3. Begin to braid the three threads. As you braid, think about the transition you are undergoing (or the transition you wish would happen).

4. When you are done braiding a cord, tie off the end.

5. Say, *"Thank you, Kali-Ma, for your strength."*

6. Leave the braid near the incense until it burns down.

7. Wear the braided cord around your wrist as you move through this transition.

8. When you are on the other side of whatever is happening, burn the cord.

SPELL FOR STRENGTH

Whether we are traveling or staying home, sometimes, we all need a little boost.

YOU WILL NEED

- Whiskey
- A glass
- Honey
- Pepper

1. Assemble your ingredients. Pour a small serving of whiskey into a glass.

2. Add a teaspoon of honey. Stir clockwise, saying, *"Kali, fortify me for what lies ahead."*

3. Sprinkle a pinch of pepper into the beverage.

4. Before you drink, say, *"Kali-Ma, I drink to you. You are strong, and I would be, too."*

5. Drink it slowly, or shoot it down. Either way, know that you have ingested some of Kali's infamous strength.

6. Only use this spell in *extreme* circumstances.

SPELL TO OVERCOME DESTRUCTION

When everything is falling apart, ask Kali to help you salvage what you need.

YOU WILL NEED

- Paper
- A pen
- A safe container to burn in
- Matches

1. Before you begin, say, *"Kali, things in my life have been destroyed. I know that destruction gives way to growth: please help me find where to start. I am ready to grow."*

2. Write down what you have lost or describe that which has been destroyed. It can be a long or a short list: it doesn't matter.

3. Crumple the paper into a loose ball. Put it in the center of your burning container (a cast iron cauldron works wonders).

4. Say, *"With this smoke, I am purified. With this flame, I am ready to move on."*

5. Light the paper. Watch it burn.

6. Toss the ashes into the toilet when the fire is done. Say, *"Kali, Great Destroyer, thank you for the gift of a new start."*

Note: *Do not attempt this spell* before *you feel that you have lost things. Kali works in strange ways, and if you call her attention before any destruction has occurred, she may decide you need a shake-up.*

$\mathcal{I}_{sis}$

Titles: Queen of Heaven, Great Mother, Divine One, Lady of Magic, Lady of Ten Thousand Names

Attributes: Magic, Self-Actualization, Royalty, Power, Devotion, Motherhood, Love, Complex Relationships

Colors: Blue, Red, Gold

Animals: Birds, Snakes

Culture of Origin: Egypt

Not to play favorites, but, well, I've got a thing for Isis. Although her worship peaked in ancient Egypt, the cult of Isis was spread all over the world through the conquering Roman empire. This goddess may possibly have Nubian origins, but she's truly an everyman and everywoman's goddess: in the ancient world, her worship demanded little in the way of class or money, and she became a favorite among slaves and royalty alike. The last Cleopatra, arguably one of the most famous rulers of Egypt, considered herself to be both the daughter of Isis and the earthly manifestation of this goddess. This multifaceted goddess is ideal for most magical workings, which makes sense, considering she is the mistress of magic.

Isis gained her magical powers in a less than exemplary way. She tricked the sun god Ra into revealing all his secrets to her after he had been bitten by a poisonous snake. In some accounts, Isis even created the snake. If he wanted to live, Ra would have to give his sneaky adoptive daughter access to his most secret spells. Ra had no choice but to share his power, elevating Isis to the top of the Egyptian pantheon with her husband Osiris.

In her aspect as wife, Isis exhibited not only passion but loyalty and dedication as well, which led her to be considered the ideal partner. Isis and Osiris ruled together for a time, but Osiris's brother Set was jealous. Set trapped Osiris and sent him to the farthest corner of the earth, but Isis found him and brought him home. Set tried again, this time dismembering his brother and scattering the pieces. Doggedly, Isis found them all. With her magic, she revived her husband and conceived a son, Horus, who would one day avenge his father. Because of the strict rules of balance in the Egyptian universe, however, Osiris was not allowed to remain with the living. He took his place as king of the dead, while Isis raised Horus and ruled over the living.

Her son opened up the third primary attribute of Isis, that of motherhood. Although we might question the parenting techniques that led her to raise her son with no other goal but to murder his uncle, there can be no doubt that Isis adored Horus. In fact, the iconic image of the mother and child that still permeates Christian worship originated with ancient statuary of Isis and Horus.

Although Isis may not be the most morally upright goddess in this book, her passion and strength tip the balance of her flaws. This is one independent goddess: she's self-actualized, and she's not afraid to take extreme measures to protect herself and the ones she loves. Is it any wonder she's still one of the most popular global goddesses?

Work with Isis before you travel, and she can offer you both protection and eye-opening experiences. As mistress of magic she can assist you when you are seeking to strengthen your spiritual and magical activities, and Isis is also an excellent figure to turn to in times of familial crisis. This goddess is a rich resource of energy just waiting to be tapped!

SPELL FOR SAFE TRAVELS

Isis went all over the world in search of her husband. The next time you leave home, let her help you.

YOU WILL NEED

- A long piece of red thread
- Scissors

1. Take the thread. Cut it so that it's long enough to wrap around your wrist at least once (more if you like).

2. As you cut the thread, say, *"Mother Isis, I ask that you watch over me as I travel _____."*

3. Tie the thread around your wrist.

4. Wear it for the entire duration of your trip. On your last day of travel, break the thread with a sharp tug and leave it outside somewhere.

SPELL FOR INCREASED AWARENESS

Whether you are traveling or at home, Isis can help you to keep an open mind. Be receptive to possibilities wherever you are.

YOU WILL NEED

- A scarf or piece of fabric (Blue is preferable.)
- A candle (Any color will do.)
- Matches
- A dark room

1. Assemble your tools.

2. Turn off the lights.

3. Place the scarf over your head, letting it hang in front of your eyes like a veil.

4. Say, *"Isis, I ask that you open my sight. Let me see the beauty all around me."*

5. Carefully, light the candle.

6. Sit quietly in the candlelight. Your eyes can be open, but keep the veil on. Don't judge your thoughts: anything that passes through your mind is worth thinking.

7. When you feel ready, take off your veil. Say, *"My world is filled with light."*

8. Blow the candle out.

SPELL FOR FINDING

If Isis could find Osiris twice, she can help you find anything you are seeking, from keys to a purpose.

YOU WILL NEED

- A bell or chime (Tapping on a pot works fine.)
- A piece of red thread at least the length of your arm (Ribbon or yarn is fine.)
- A small object that symbolizes the thing you want to find

1. Ring the bell once. Say, *"Isis, help me find _____."*

2. Tie the red thread to the object. Knot the thread nine times.

3. Hang the thread on your front door (from the doorknob is ideal).

4. Ring the bell once. Say, *"Isis, lend me your magic."*

5. Every time you leave or enter your home, touch the thread and be reminded that your spell is working.

6. Once you find the thing you are looking for, untie the thread. Set the object in a small dish of salt to cleanse it, or throw it away. Dispose of the thread.

Hecate

Titles: Queen of Witches, Triple Lady, Keeper of Darkness, She Who Walks Between Worlds, Goddess of the Crossroads

Attributes: Thresholds, Transition, Magic, Death, Triple Goddess, Crossroads

Color: Black

Animals: Dogs, Especially Hounds

Culture of Origin: Possibly Anatolia/Pre-Greek/Hellenistic

Hecate is often depicted as a dark, fearsome crone, but she actually embodies three goddess archetypes: maiden, mother, and crone. Images of Hecate from antiquity show us a three-headed goddess, a woman with the ability to consider all options while looking forward and making a clear decision. Like Brigid, Hecate is a triple goddess, and as such, she has a wide range of powers, including guidance through transitions, witchcraft, and protection. When this Anatolian goddess migrated into first Greek and then Roman cultures, she brought with her the wisdom of dark places that many people fear to this day.

In the Greek story of Demeter and Persephone, Hecate is the only deity who is willing to defy Zeus and tell Demeter what happened to Persephone when she went missing. Later, when Hades and Demeter strike an uneasy accord, Hecate accompanies Persephone on her journeys to and from the underworld. Hecate is one of a handful of Greco-Roman figures who is permitted access to the realm of Hades, and it is in this guise as intermediary for the dead that she became popularized in late medieval Christian Europe.

When William Shakespeare penned *Macbeth*, he immortalized Hecate as the queen of darkness and ruler of witchcraft. Hecate has always been a goddess of the shadows, and her continued association with magical rites has made her a popular figure with witches and magicians over the centuries.

But there's another side to Hecate. In some stories, she is named as one of the Titans, the race that Zeus and the other Olympians overthrew in their own rise to power. As such, Hecate is said to be the only Titan honored on Mount Olympus, so much so that Zeus asked her to watch over his children. Some even say that he gave her a singular power; Hecate was allowed to give or take anything she chose from the mortals on earth, and no god was allowed to stop her.

Clearly, this lady of darkness is a powerful goddess. Although it's hard to know her because of the conflicting stories that have sprung up over the years, that's just part of Hecate's charm: as a goddess of thresholds, she represents that which is intangible, even spectral. If we could pin her down and define her, she wouldn't be true to her own essence.

Work with Hecate when you are seeking protection, especially from unseen forces. You can also seek her advice when you find yourself standing at a crossroads; she won't tell you which path to choose, for she values free will, but she may help you to see your options with more clarity. She's also a great goddess to work with if you want to learn methods of divination or seeing the future. Let Hecate shine her torch into your life, but don't expect coddling from this powerful, dark goddess: she values those who value themselves.

SPELL FOR MENTAL PROTECTION

Sometimes, you need shielding from the thoughts and words of those around you. Hecate can offer shelter!

YOU WILL NEED

- An empty jar or bottle with a lid
- Salt
- Basil
- Olive oil
- A bathtub
- Candles and matches (optional)

1. Pour salt into the jar or bottle. Say, *"Salt purifies my mind. Let me keep my thoughts clear."*

2. Add the basil leaves to the jar. Say, *"Basil is for protection. Let me keep my thoughts safe."*

3. Pour the olive oil over the salt and basil, filling the jar halfway. Seal it, and shake the mixture, saying, *"Hecate, watch over me."*

4. Run a hot bath. As the water is running, pour most of the oil mixture under the stream. Leave some in the jar.

5. Light candles if you want, but turn off the bathroom light.

6. Once you are in the tub, pour the rest of the oil between your hands. Say, *"With this spell I keep my thoughts well."*

7. Close your eyes and smooth your cupped hands over your forehead and back over your hair to the nape of your neck.

8. Soak as long as you want to.

9. After the tub is drained, take a quick shower. Rinse out the tub, using a tissue to catch any basil leaves. Flush these remnants down the toilet.

SPELL FOR CHOICES

Sometimes, we feel crippled when we are faced with a choice. Use this spell to come to a final decision when you are torn between two or three things.

YOU WILL NEED

- Three uncooked spaghetti or fettuccini noodles (same length)

1. Sit in a quiet, dark room with the three noodles arranged in front of you. Say, *"Goddess of the Crossroads, I am struggling with a choice. Please help me find an answer."*

2. Touch the first noodle. Say, *"This symbolizes a choice: it is_____."*

3. Repeat step 2 with the other noodles. If you are only choosing between two things, when you get to the third noodle, say, *"This symbolizes the possibility of the unknown."*

4. Start with the first noodle. Lift it up. Think about the choice. What are the cons to this choice? Each time you think of a con, say it out loud and snap off a small piece of the noodle.

5. Repeat step 4 with choices two and three.

6. Turn on the lights. Which noodle is the shortest? That's the one you want the least.

7. Which noodle is the longest? That symbolizes the choice you want the most.

8. If you don't like the way the noodles ended up, well, that gives you an answer, too!

9. Whichever choice you make, step forward with confidence.

SPELL FOR INTUITION

Have you ever wished you could tap into your intuitive powers and gain guidance from the cosmos? This spell will help you get started.

YOU WILL NEED

- Either a tarot deck or a set of runes
- A purple candle
- Matches
- A notebook and something to write with

1. Set your divination tool on the floor. Sit comfortably in front of it.

2. Light the purple candle and say, *"Hecate, I wish to learn the art of seeing with my heart."*

3. Begin to play with the cards or runes. Shuffle them, jangle them, spread them out, mix them up. Do whatever you want for a while.

4. At random, pull a card or a rune.

5. Set it in front of the candle where you can see it clearly.

6. Taking your writing implement and notebook, take down information about the card or rune. Draw it. Describe it. What do you see?

7. Now, write down your emotional reactions: What do you feel? Does it remind you of anything?

8. Work through as many cards or runes as you like. When you are exhausted, pack everything up with care. Remember, these are your tools: treat them well!

9. Before you snuff out the candle with your fingertips, say, *"I may not be there yet, but I have begun."*

10. Repeat the spell until you feel comfortable with your divination tool. You can refer to the guidebook that came with your cards or runes, but trust your instincts and let Hecate guide you.

Artemis

Titles: Lady of Beasts, Many-Breasted One, Virgin Huntress, Lady of the Moon

Attributes: Hunting, Stewardship, Virginity, Modesty, Maternity, Pregnancy, Fertility, Animals, the Moon

Colors: White, Blue, Black, Yellow

Animals: Dogs, Especially Hunting Hounds, Bears, All Wild Animals

Culture of Origin: Pre-Greek/Hellenistic

Artemis is tough stuff. When this goddess was born, her mother Leto was still laboring to deliver Artemis's twin, Apollo. Infant Artemis got down to business and served as her mother's midwife, cementing her place among goddesses as one who will do anything to ease the pains of childbirth.

Despite her continued role in all matters of maternity, Artemis is not a motherly goddess. This feisty goddess begged her father Zeus to never force her to marry, and she remained a blissful maiden. There was that brief affair with her mortal hunting buddy Orion, but when he ended up dead, Artemis reverted to her celibate ways, running around the woods free and unencumbered. It's in this guise, as the Virgin Huntress, that she is most well-known in the modern world. But don't think of her as an innocent child: this goddess can certainly hold her own!

Take, for example, the case of Actaeon. The idiot decided he wanted to sneak a peek at Artemis while she was bathing by moonlight one night, so he headed out to the woods with his hunting dogs, eager to track the elusive goddess. Eventually, he found her, and got quite an eyeful. Artemis heard him panting in the bushes and immediately retaliated by turning him into a stag. Maybe the goddess planned to hunt him down, but Actaeon's own dogs beat her to the punch, and the deer formerly known as Actaeon was murdered. The lesson? When a woman says no, she means it!

Her legendary fierceness may seem an odd contrast to her maternal protection of animals and women in childbirth, but there's a certain sort of violence in love that we often ignore. Love is a raw, powerful emotion, and Artemis typifies that energy. She culls her own herds through hunting, but the Greeks also told tales of Artemis turning her arrows on hunters who dared to kill pregnant animals or their children. She never had children of her own, and yet women in childbirth have called on her for centuries to hold their hands and ease their pain.

Artemis is a strong goddess, and she continues to present a comprehensive image of what a powerful woman can be. Call on this goddess when you are feeling fragile or threatened, and she will leap to your aid. But don't call her for petty slights or minor concerns: Artemis doesn't like to be trifled with, and you may find yourself on the receiving end of her wrath if you seek her help without real need. Whenever you are truly frightened, Artemis can help. She's an especially good goddess to work with if you've suffered sexual or emotional abuse, so turn to her when you need the energy to overcome personal tragedy. Borrow her strength and learn how to take back your life.

SPELL FOR RECOVERY

If you've been the victim of abuse, use this spell to begin the healing process.

YOU WILL NEED

- A bathtub
- Dried sage
- Matches
- A fire-safe dish
- Salt

1. Begin to fill the tub with hot water.

2. Light the sage. Say, *"Artemis, huntress, help me to find my inner strength. Please help me put the past firmly in the past."*

3. Leave the sage burning on a fire-safe dish on the edge of the tub. Ease yourself into the water (which should still be running).

4. Fill your hands with salt.

5. Scoop the salt over your head, allowing it to trickle into the water. Say, *"By this action, I am cleansed. By smoke and salt and by your will, Artemis, I am ready to be whole."*

6. Once the tub fills, turn off the water. Soak as long as you need to. You might feel tears building up: this is a safe place to cry. Don't censor yourself.

7. When you are done with the bath, drain the tub. Wrap yourself in a soft towel and say, *"Artemis, by your bow and by your moon, I grow strong again."*

8. Repeat nightly for a week if needed.

SPELL FOR SELF-PRIDE

Sometimes, loving ourselves gets harder over time. Let Artemis help you see your own unique strength and beauty.

YOU WILL NEED

- An appointment at a hair salon (preferably a place you've been before)

1. Before you leave the house for your haircut, spend five minutes looking into the mirror. What do you love about

yourself? Say, *"I love my _____."* List all the things that you love about yourself.

2. At the hair salon, either find a picture in one of their style guides that you want to try, or simply trust the stylist. Make a drastic change, whether it's cut, color, style, or all of the above.

3. When you get home, look in the mirror again. Say, *"Like you, Artemis, I am renewed. I love this new look. I love myself."*

4. This spell is a great pick-me-up whenever you feel flat. There's nothing wrong with a little practical renewal: Artemis understands the need to feel comfortable in your skin.

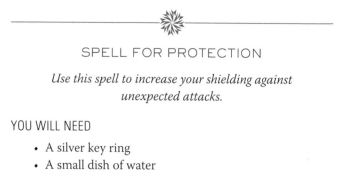

SPELL FOR PROTECTION

Use this spell to increase your shielding against unexpected attacks.

YOU WILL NEED

- A silver key ring
- A small dish of water
- A full moon

1. On the night before the moon is full (this is easy enough to check on your calendar or online), take the silver key ring and the small dish of water outside. If you don't have a yard or a porch, you can do this in a windowsill.

2. Hold the key ring up to the moon. Say, *"With this charm, I harness the power of the moon. Watch over me, Artemis, and keep me from harm."*

3. Drop the key ring in the dish of water.

4. Leave the dish outside (or on the windowsill) in the moonlight.

5. The next night, when the moon is full, lift the dish up to the sky and say, *"I charge this charm with the light of the moon. The power of Artemis will always be within my reach."*

6. Leave the dish outside in the moonlight again.

7. On the third night, dump the water out in your garden or on a houseplant. Put your keys on the key ring, and carry it with you.

Note: *No spell can replace safety precautions and your instincts, so make sure you still remain aware of your surroundings if you are out after dark, and always tell someone where you are going.*

Gaia

Titles: Earth Mother, Great One, Lady of the Mountains, Mother of All

Attributes: Fertility, Maternity, Independence, Protection, Family

Colors: Green, Blue, Brown

Animals: Bear, Fox, Hawk

Culture of Origin: Pre-Greek/Hellenistic

Gaia is an incredibly popular goddess: you see her name and image everywhere! She's literally the earth beneath our feet, and even people who've never heard the word "goddess" use Gaia's name to talk about our home planet. Despite her popularity, Gaia is a fairly ill-treated goddess. It isn't hard to look around and find examples of abuse against her: trash beside the highway, pollution in the streams, unsafe mining practices, and the list goes on.

You might wonder why Gaia sits back and takes all this from humanity, but you have to remember that she's a mother. She's so used to being taken for granted by her children that it's only in rare cases that she thinks of herself and tries to fight back. Her first husband, the sky god Uranus, grew jealous of Gaia's many children and forced her to keep some of them locked away within herself. You try telling a new mother to put her baby back in her womb and see where that gets you. Gaia bided her time, but eventually, when her son Cronus was born, she handed him a sickle and told him to castrate his father. You don't want to mess with Mama Gaia!

Even as Cronus and the other Titans fell to the Olympian gods, Gaia remained unchangeable and ever present. In ancient Greece, both gods and mortals would make sacred oaths in Gaia's name, binding themselves in their promises to the power of the earth. As the earth mother, Gaia is abundantly fertile, and not all of her children are godly and glorious. Gaia mothered monsters as well as Titans, but she guarded all of her children with the fierce protectiveness that is so stereotypical of mothers.

Gaia is more than just a mother, though. Her prophetess may have been the first to speak in the voice of the Delphic oracle, and one story tells that Apollo killed Gaia's great python to gain control of the oracle for himself. Hera punished him (possibly saving him from whatever nasty fate Gaia wanted to dish up), but the oracle changed hands. Even so, Gaia is still associated with the gift of prophecy. She's a great goddess to talk to if you are struggling to catch a glimpse of your future.

Gaia's ability to reproduce makes her a favorite figure among farmers and gardeners, but even if you don't have a green thumb, Gaia can help you find bounty in your life. Use the spells in this section to help you produce healthy food (whether bought or grown), and work with Gaia  whenever you feel a little ungrounded. This earthy goddess always delivers a fast reality check, but even as she whacks you upside the head, Gaia opens her arms to shelter you. She is the mother of all mothers.

SPELL FOR GROWTH

If you feel like you need to boost your personal development, let Gaia lend a hand.

YOU WILL NEED

- A dried bean (any kind)
- A small piece of cotton (preferably undyed)
- A needle
- Green thread

1. Set the bean on the piece of fabric. Say, *"Gaia, I am seeking growth in this area of my life: _____."*

2. Thread the needle.

3. Fold in the corners of the fabric on the diagonal, bringing all four corners together in the center.

4. Begin to sew the corners together. As you work, think about the ways you are hoping to grow.

5. Sew the edges until you've made a little bag for the bean. Tie off the thread with three knots and say, *"Gaia, thank you for watching over this seed of my growth."*

6. Keep the charm close to you: leave it under your pillow or put it in your car.

7. When the growth you have looked for begins to sprout, bury the charm in a flowerpot or your backyard.

SPELL FOR SUSTENANCE

Whether you want to grow a garden, cook good meals, or find cheap takeout, we all want to be well-fed. Let Gaia help you.

YOU WILL NEED

- Five pennies (the shinier, the better)
- A small terra-cotta pot
- Dirt

1. Drop the pennies into the pot one at a time. With each penny, say, *"Gaia, grant that I never hunger."*

2. Scoop a handful of dirt over the pennies. Say, *"I set my intention to (learn to garden, learn to cook, learn to find good food)."*

3. Scoop a second handful of dirt into the pot. Say, *"With Gaia, I will always have enough."*

4. Scoop a third handful into the pot. Say, *"Full belly, full pot, full heart."*

5. Leave the penny pot in a bright, sunny place. (A kitchen windowsill is best.)

SPELL FOR PROTECTION

Gaia's sheltering powers are vast: she is always there, wherever you are.

YOU WILL NEED

- Comfortable shoes
- Somewhere to walk

1. Lace up your shoes and head out. Make sure you tell someone where you are going and how long you plan to be gone. (This ritual can be done in about five minutes, but you can extend the walk as long as you want.)

2. As you walk, watch your feet. Look at what you step on. Is there any garbage you can pick up? Or perhaps you see something that wants to become your talisman. If you stop to pick up anything (garbage or gift), say, *"Gaia is beneath me."*

3. Keep walking. Feel the strength of the ground underneath your feet. Marvel at how Gaia supports you.

4. Whenever you are done walking and in sight of your dwelling place, stop for a moment. Say, *"As long as I am on the earth, I am protected."* Feel Gaia's protection seeping through the soles of your shoes, into your legs, up your torso, and all the way to the crown of your head.

5. Repeat this spell whenever you are feeling shaky or ungrounded.

CHAPTER 5

Too Much of a Good Thing?

I have to run to the post office today and pay the bills. The cat's out of her flea treatment, and my husband needs to stay late at work. Then we've got friends coming over for dinner. And that's just today: in this week alone, I have a coffee date, two dinner dates, a writing group, and a spiritual retreat to attend. Life gets busy fast, and most of the time, I let it overwhelm me.

But last spring when I was at a group meeting for a local organization, I started to voice my crazy, hectic schedule to the woman standing beside me. "I just don't know how I'm going to do it all!"

She smiled. "You'll find a way. You are so blessed: look at all the abundance in your life!"

My first impulse was to smack her. There I was, on the verge of a nervous breakdown, and Ms. Pollyanna was telling me that my stressors were actually blessings.

Before I could start a fight, I stopped and really thought about what she'd said. Sure, my life is busy, but isn't that because of the choices I've made? If I'm being honest with myself, I thrive on a little bit of chaos, and my lifestyle supplies just the right dose. But abundance? I scoffed at that idea. Abundance means money and possessions, right? I certainly don't have a surplus of either.

But there's more to abundance than that, as my companion recognized that day. Sure, money is nice, and it's fun to have a pair of diamond earrings for every day of the week, but these things are just the tip of the abundance iceberg. When I stopped to look for it, I realized that my life is overflowing. I have abundant joy and laughter with my husband, and our friends and family fill our lives with energy and adventure. Even the way I choose to spend my time is a measure of my bounty: I can curl up on the couch for an evening and read a delicious novel, even if that means that tomorrow I'll have to work a little harder to meet my responsibilities.

Every culture has valued abundance differently, and the different goddesses in this section illustrate the diversity of the idea of wealth. Lakshmi is the Hindu goddess of wealth and luck, but she also dabbles in matters of the heart. Kuan Yin has a surplus of kindness and charity, something which she passes on to all who say her name. Lusty Hathor, the cow-headed goddess of the Egyptian pantheon, loves lovers, music, and revelry. Then there's Demeter, the prolific mother of the harvest who makes sure we always have enough to eat. Fortuna is literally Lady Luck, so if you'd care to take a gamble, she's your girl. Use the spells in this section to cultivate abundance in a variety of areas in your life, and remember: it's not just about tangible wealth. Abundance is more, well, abundant than that.

Lakshmi

Titles: Lady of the Lotus, Luck-Bringer, Wealthy One

Attributes: Luck, Wealth, Beauty, Abundance

Colors: Pink, Blue, Orange, Red, White, Yellow

Animals: Elephant, Cow

Culture of Origin: India (Hindu)

Like the Hellenistic Aphrodite, Lakshmi's origin is mysterious and romantic. When the gods began to churn the primordial sea, searching for a way to preserve their immortality, Lakshmi floated to the surface of the strange, milky water, riding a lotus blossom and radiant in her beauty. Because of her presence, the gods were able to tip the balance in their favor in the constant struggle against demons; Lakshmi brought love and light to the Hindu pantheon, and she's a much beloved goddess.

After her bizarre birth, Lakshmi took up residence as the consort of the god Vishnu. The Hindu deities take on many forms and incarnations, and paired with Vishnu, Lakshmi seems to have reincarnated constantly. However, no matter which form she took, she always brought wealth and blessings with her. Lakshmi is also seen as a mother goddess, although she does not have associations with physical fertility. Lakshmi's blessings are physical treasures, and her images often show gold coins flowing from her hands. She's a fountain of wealth!

As the bringer of material wealth, Lakshmi's worship is widespread. Businesses and homes have shrines to her, but the goddess knows the difference between greed and need. It is believed that Lakshmi rewards those of her devotees who work hard and consistently strive to improve their lives: this is one goddess of luck who believes that we make our own luck! It's hard not to love this beautiful, abundant goddess.

Working magic with Lakshmi is fun. This goddess loves laughter and sunlight, and her assistance will brighten your life even if you don't need material wealth. Just remember that Lakshmi likes strong women who are willing to work for what they want; if you take the first steps, Lakshmi will propel you on your journey. She's also a good goddess to turn to for matters of the heart. Her relationship with Vishnu is filled with passion and joy, and Lakshmi loves to spread warm fuzzies around.

The bottom line with this goddess is that she takes great joy out of providing pleasure. If you're feeling a little pinched financially, or if you want a boost of positive energy in your life, try the spells in this section. Working magic with Lakshmi is heady stuff: just remember to come back down to earth after you hang out with this effervescent goddess.

SPELL FOR PROSPERITY

If you want to ensure that you will always have enough, let Lakshmi be your guide.

YOU WILL NEED

- A silver coin (Quarters work best.)
- A piece of pink silk

1. Hold the coin in your right hand and the silk in your left hand.

2. Say, *"Lakshmi, Lady of the Lotus, I ask your blessings upon my wealth. May it always increase as my needs increase, and may my cash flow never run dry."*

3. Wrap the coin in the silk.

4. Carry the silk-wrapped coin in your wallet.

5. If you feel like your earning power needs a boost, take out the silk-wrapped coin on the night of the full moon and leave it in a windowsill to recharge. Return it to your wallet the next morning.

SPELL FOR LAUGHTER

Sometimes, our greatest wealth is a good laugh. Ask Lakshmi for help when you find it hard to smile.

YOU WILL NEED

- Metal wind chimes
- A sunny day

1. Decide if you will hang the chimes inside or outside. Hang a hook wherever you want the chimes.

2. Set the chimes outside at noon on a sunny day. Say, *"Lakshmi, fill my life with laughter and joy."*

3. Leave the chimes outside for two or three hours.

4. Pick up the chimes and hang them up. Say, *"Laughter is magical music. Lakshmi watches over me."*

5. Every time the chimes ring, know that the goddess is laughing nearby.

SPELL FOR LUCK

When you take a risk, let Lakshmi infuse your action with luck.

YOU WILL NEED
- A scratch-off lottery ticket
- A penny

1. Hold the lottery ticket and penny. Say, *"Luck is with me because Lakshmi is with me. I believe in luck."*

2. Slowly, use the penny to scratch off the ticket.

3. Hang it on your fridge. Every time you look at it, remember that Lakshmi is working to bring luck into your life.

GODDESS SPELLS FOR BUSY GIRLS

Kuan Yin

Titles: Goddess of Mercy, Enlightened One,
Lady of Grace

Attributes: Peace, Tranquility, Sacrifice,
Compassion, Transcendence

Color: White

Animals: Dove, Wildcat, Fish

Culture of Origin: China (Buddhist)

This beloved bodhisattva isn't technically a goddess, but she's
as close as you can get in Buddhism. Once a mortal woman,
Kuan Yin was martyred by her father when she wished to join
a convent and dedicate herself to spirituality. This martyrdom
set her on the path of enlightenment, but unlike other figures
in Buddhism, Kuan Yin turned back when nirvana was within
her reach. Although she was spiritually
prepared to leave the earth and become
pure energy, Kuan Yin declared that she
would stay put until all women and men
attained enlightenment. She's been stuck
on earth ever since, but her caring nature hasn't diminished.
At her core, Kuan Yin is selfless and loving, dedicated to help-
ing mortals find their hearts' desires.

Kuan Yin has stepped beyond the boundaries of Chinese
Buddhism and is sometimes associated with the Virgin Mary.
Both are figures of quiet sacrifice, and both are powerful ex-
amples of female divinity. It is said that simply speaking Kuan

Yin's name will ensure her attention, and this ever-abundant goddess fulfills all prayers that are addressed to her. She's often shown holding a vessel, which represents the grace that she pours out for humanity, and she's usually depicted sitting on a lotus blossom: this is the standard symbol for enlightenment in many eastern mythologies.

Talk to this goddess whenever you are feeling overwhelmed by life. She's always willing to listen, and Kuan Yin never judges anyone. This all-accepting, all-loving goddess is very helpful when you are seeking emotional fulfillment. Kuan Yin possesses an abundance of patience and compassion, and the spells in this section are ideal for times when you feel that you are lacking either of these attributes. Let Kuan Yin guide you through the fraught holiday seasons, or turn to her when you are feeling ragged and need a safe place to recharge.

Kuan Yin doesn't ask for much in return, but try to keep in mind the example she sets when you are feeling down and out. The world isn't wonderful, but sometimes, there are wonderful people (and goddesses) willing to stick around during tough times. To say thanks to her after a spell, simply repeat her beautiful name!

SPELL FOR PATIENCE

This is one virtue that most of us don't have enough of. Let Kuan Yin help you cultivate patience, even when times get tough!

YOU WILL NEED

- Two empty bowls
- A cup of uncooked rice

1. Find a comfortable place to sit. Set the empty bowls and the cup of rice in front of you.

2. Say, *"Kuan Yin, Kuan Yin, Kuan Yin, help me cultivate patience. I do not want to rush through my life. Make me aware."*

3. One grain of rice at a time, place the rice first in one bowl, then the other.

4. When the bowls of rice are full, hold one up and say, *"Kuan Yin, I give you this rice in thanks."*

5. Dump all the rice into a rice cooker or pot, and serve it for dinner. As you eat, know that you are ingesting patience.

SPELL FOR COMPASSION

Use this spell whenever you just can't see eye to eye with someone. This is especially useful in election years!

YOU WILL NEED

- A sheet of paper
- Something to write with

1. Say, *"Kuan Yin, help me find common ground with (name of the person)."*

2. Think of the person in question. What do the two of you have in common? Write down everything that comes to mind.

3. When you think you've come up with everything, try to add three more items to your list.

4. Say, *"Kuan Yin, let me show compassion to _____. He/ she is like me in so many ways. This is what we share in common: _____"* and read your list out loud.

5. Put the list somewhere unobtrusive but easily accessible. Whenever you find your compassion slipping, take out the list and read it out loud again.

SPELL FOR EMOTIONAL ABUNDANCE

Have you ever felt drained and emotionally exhausted? Use this spell to get your mojo back.

YOU WILL NEED

- A white candle (vanilla-scented is ideal)
- A bathtub
- Rose- or patchouli-scented bubble bath

1. Light the candle. Say, *"Kuan Yin, please help me replenish my heart."*

2. Run the bath. As the tub fills with hot water, add the scented bubble bath.

3. When the tub is full, carry the candle to the edge of the tub. Turn off the water and get in.

4. Close your eyes. Take a deep breath.

5. Hold your breath for a count of five.

6. Exhale.

7. Repeat steps 4 through 6 three times.

8. Open your eyes. Say, *"With Kuan Yin's help, my heart is full."*

9. Stay in the tub as long as you want.

10. When you are done, blow out the candle and drain the tub.

11. Repeat this spell whenever you feel frayed.

Hathor

Titles: Bountiful One, Great Cow, Great Consort, Mistress of Music

Attributes: Music, Dance, Revelry, Lust, Sexual Pleasure, Beauty, Solar Energy

Colors: Red, Orange, Yellow, Bright Blue, Pink

Animal: Cow

Culture of Origin: Egypt

Although this goddess is frequently depicted as a cow, there's nothing slow or plodding about her. Hathor is the goddess of fertility, abundance, and pleasure in the Egyptian pantheon, and her favors were enjoyed by the common folk of Egypt and the pharaohs for centuries. Although she later merged with Isis, Hathor is a distinct goddess, powerful in her own right.

She is one of the many goddesses considered to be "the eye of Ra," and in some mythologies, she's said to be Ra's wife, as well. Later stories have her married to Horus, the son of Isis, and still others list Hathor as Horus's mother. The many faces of this goddess are hard to keep track of, but the bottom line is that Hathor was a popular goddess, promising her worshipers all manner of earthly pleasures. It's no wonder that her annual festival was a rollicking party!

In her form of the great celestial cow, some stories tell of Hathor giving birth to the universe. Her animal image was hugely popular in ancient Egypt, and it's not uncommon to find artwork depicting this or that pharaoh being suckled by the great cow. Because of this, Hathor has maternal connections, and it was believed that she offered protection to all pregnant and nursing mothers.

Many temples sprang up in Egypt dedicated to this goddess, and her face still appears on the pillars and ruins up and down the Nile. With Hathor watching over you, it's guaranteed that your life will be filled with music and merriment. Her priestesses were considered experts in the arts of love and entertainment, and the Greeks confused Hathor with their own lusty goddess Aphrodite. Her temples were pleasure palaces, overflowing with all kinds of tangible abundance.

Hathor was also fond of foreigners, and for a time in Egyptian history, she was portrayed as the queen of the dead. This welcoming goddess never turned anybody away, even if the person was no longer in possession of a body. Celebrations honoring Hathor involved sweet cakes and beer, and music pulsed in the streets for days. It's interesting to note that Hathor is the tamed aspect of the fierce goddess Sekhmet: when Hathor became enraged, she transformed into the lion-headed goddess, but when Sekhmet was tricked with red beer, Hathor's calm demeanor once again took over. This myth reminds us that passionate indulgence is closely linked to fury, and it doesn't take much for a party to turn into something dangerous.

Use the spells in this section to give your life an infusion of passion and fun. Hathor wants you to get your groove on, so go out there and make music, love, or some other kind of revelry. Don't let her cow eyes fool you: this goddess knows how to have a good time.

SPELL FOR A GOOD TIME

Heading out on the town? Let Hathor make your night sparkle!

YOU WILL NEED

- A group of friends (It's more fun to travel in a pack!)
- Somewhere to go that has music (Dancing is a plus.)
- Money for a cab
- Dark eyeliner (or glittery eye shadow)
- A sparkly top

1. Set up a girls' night out with your friends. Pick a place, make a plan, and make sure everyone has enough for a cab ride home.

2. Before the big night, apply eyeliner to your eyes. Remember what Liz Taylor looked like in *Cleopatra*? Not quite that much, but come close. Make a statement.

3. After your eyes are done, look in the mirror. Say, *"Hathor, fill my night with music. Let me rejoice and find pleasure tonight."*

4. Don your sparkly top. You are beautiful, confident, and glorious!

5. Go out. Have fun! Stick with your girls, and don't drive home.

6. Before you collapse into bed, wash off your eyeliner. Say, *"Thank you, Hathor, for letting me borrow your sparkle tonight."*

SPELL FOR LETTING LOOSE

Do you feel like you can't ever relax enough to have fun? Let Hathor remove your inhibitions temporarily.

YOU WILL NEED

- A bathtub
- Rose-scented bath oil
- A washable marker (any color)

1. Fill the tub with hot water.

2. Add the bath oil. Say, *"Hathor, unlock my inhibitions. Let me be free."*

3. Settle into the tub for a long soak.

4. After your bath, dry off. Pick a spot on your body that will be covered by clothing.

5. Use the washable marker to draw either an ankh (it looks like a cross with a round head), or a pair of cow horns around a circle. It can be small or large, intricate or simple, but it must be hidden somewhere that only you know about.

6. Say, *"Hathor, I walk in your footsteps. I am no longer confined."*

7. Even once the symbol has washed off during your next shower or bath, know that the magic is continuing to work.

8. Don't repeat this spell too often: remember, there can be too much of a good thing.

SPELL FOR A GREAT DATE

Whether it's your first or your thousandth, use this spell to make sure you have a wonderful time with your sweetie.

YOU WILL NEED
- A recording of your favorite song(s)
- A piece of gold jewelry

1. As you get ready for your date, put your music on. Draw the curtains and dance around your room. No one is watching!

2. Get dressed and prepped.

3. Put on the gold jewelry last. Say, *"Hathor, let this date be remarkable. I want an evening (morning, afternoon) to remember. Fill our hearts with joy and laughter."*

4. Go out with your sweetie (or just stay in), and keep the gold jewelry on until you are ready for the date to end (even if you aren't wearing anything else by then!).

$\mathcal{D}$emeter

Titles: Grain Mother, Great Mother, Abundant One

Attributes: Fertility, Motherhood, Harvest, Grain, Apples, Grapes, Honey

Colors: Gold, Green, Brown, Red

Animal: Pig

Culture of Origin: Pre-Greek/Hellenistic

The greatest ritual initiation in the ancient world took place at Eleusis. Every year, thousands of people made the trip to participate in the sacred ceremony. Although parts of the ceremony were public, the final steps of initiation were conducted in secret. Despite the number of people who participated, no one ever revealed the secret to a noninitiate: the rites of Demeter were that powerful.

The Eleusinian Mysteries were based on the central myth of Demeter, goddess of the abundant harvest. She was the mother of Persephone, whom you've already encountered in chapter 2. When Persephone went missing, Demeter was driven mad with grief. She roamed the earth weeping, but she could find no sign of her beloved daughter. The goddess's tears turned bitter the longer her daughter was lost, and eventually, the earth itself shriveled up in sympathy. Demeter would not allow anything to grow until her daughter had been returned to her.

In this myth, we see not only a lovely explanation for the seasonal changes of the year, but also that abundance is not a guarantee. When Demeter recovered from her sadness and spent a little time with her daughter, it's said that she allowed the earth to produce again and taught some of the people who had helped her in her misery how to cultivate the earth and increase the harvest. But without Demeter's blessing, that harvest would never have been possible.

This is true in our own lives; it's often said that "It never rains but it pours." Good things tend to bombard us all at once, and the reverse is also true. Whether in abundance or want, we live our lives in cycles. Demeter's myth is at the core of one of those cycles, and she is a volatile, powerful goddess to work with.

Call on Demeter whenever you are ready to harvest things in your life: the metaphorical results of hard work and the literal plant crops are both in her jurisdiction. She can help you sort through things in your life when you are ready to make some changes, too. Demeter also understands what it's like to have your heart broken by a child, so she's a great goddess to work with for teachers, social workers, and parents. Before attempting any of the spells in this section, however, remember that Demeter's moods are changeable: if she's in a good mood, she'll aid everyone. But if you catch her on a bad day, you will wish you'd never heard her name. Be patient, but she's espe-

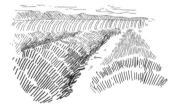

GODDESS SPELLS FOR BUSY GIRLS

cially willing to help in the late summer and early fall. Under no circumstances should you attempt a Demeter spell in the winter. She's never liked winter, since it marks the time when she lost her daughter. I don't blame her; I prefer the fall, too.

SPELL FOR HARVESTING

Do you have a project that has slowly been growing which you are finally ready to finish? Use this spell and tap into Demeter's energy to fulfill your harvest.

YOU WILL NEED

- Bouquet of brightly colored flowers (not roses)
- A vase
- An aspirin tablet

1. Snip the ends of the flowers one at a time under warm, running water. With each snip, think about the thing you are ready to harvest. What will the harvest look like? What will it sound like? What will it feel like? What will it smell like? What will it taste like?

2. Set the flowers aside.

3. Add about four inches of lukewarm water to the vase.

4. Crush an aspirin tablet and add it to the water. Say, *"Demeter, may these blooms remind me of (the project that you are ready to finish). May they be bright and bring joy into my home."*

5. Arrange the flowers in the vase. Say, *"Demeter, help me bring in my harvest. The time for growing is done; I am ready to resolve this project."*

6. Put the flowers on the center of your table, or somewhere else in your home where you will see them two or three times a day.

7. Leave the flowers out until they are withered and brown. Toss them on the compost pile and dump out the water.

8. It's time to bring in the harvest. You can finish what you've started or let go of something that you've clung to. Everything in its season!

SPELL FOR KEEPING SECRETS

If you have a hard time keeping secrets, ask Demeter for help. After all, what happened at Eleusis stayed at Eleusis!

YOU WILL NEED

- A mirror
- A gold or yellow spell candle
- Matches

1. Stand in front of the mirror (or hold it up to your face).

2. Tell yourself the secret that you are bursting to reveal: say it out loud, and watch your face in the mirror as you say it.

3. Say it again.

4. Light the candle. Say, *"This is the last time I will speak this secret until _____."* (Don't say "ever." Set a reasonable time frame on your silence.)

5. Look into the mirror and speak the secret out loud one more time.

6. As you finish speaking, blow out the candle.

7. Whenever you feel the urge to reveal the secret, light the candle and remember the vow you made.

8. When your promise is up and it's okay to reveal the secret, you may find that you are no longer bursting to share the news.

SPELL FOR SURVIVING AN EMOTIONAL FLOOD

Demeter knows all about too much of something. Use this spell to make it easier to deal with an overwhelming amount of emotions.

YOU WILL NEED

- A shower
- A warm bathrobe or pajamas

1. Let the water run as hot as you can stand before stepping into the shower.

2. Close your eyes and tilt your face toward the spray.

3. Say, *"Demeter, help me weather this storm. I am overwhelmed with good/bad things right now. Help me find a calm harbor."*

4. Keep your eyes closed. Step under the water, letting it run down your face, your head, your back, encircling your body with warmth.

5. Stand there for as long as you want.

6. As you turn off the water, open your eyes and say, *"With your help, Demeter, I can ride out this flux. This is not too much: it is just my life, and that makes it good."*

7. After you dry off, wrap yourself in a warm robe or a comfortable pair of pajamas. Try to perform this spell right before you go to bed.

8. If you have any dreams after this spell, write them down. You never know what kind of messages you might get!

Fortuna

Titles: Lady Luck

Attributes: Luck, Fate, Abundance, Cornucopia, Blindness, Fertility

Colors: Black, White, Blue, Green

Animals: Rabbit, Cat, Bluebird

Culture of Origin: Italy (Pre-Roman)

Long before Marlon Brando ever crooned to a pair of dice, the Romans had immortalized Lady Luck. Fortuna (or Fors, as she was sometimes called) governed not only luck but fertility, prosperity, and public opinion. She was often shown either blind or blindfolded, reminding folks that fortune isn't an exact science. It was believed that if you offended Fortuna in some way, you would have a lifetime of ill luck to work off before you could catch her attention again.

Fortuna made her way to Christian Europe as a symbol: the wheel of fortune isn't just a card in tarot. This concept of an ever-revolving fate grabbed hold of Europeans, and Lady Luck continued to be worshiped throughout the ages, especially by politicians and monarchs. William Shakespeare perpetuated the idea of Dame Fortuna, personifying luck and fate in a number of his plays and sonnets.

Despite her continued popularity, stories of Fortuna haven't really survived. How then can we modern girls work with

this flighty, intangible goddess? You spin the wheel, and you take your chances, folks. Working with Fortuna takes trust and acceptance that she isn't just the goddess of good fortune; she's the goddess of all fortune, period. That means you might wind up with the bad as well as the good. But that's pretty much what life is like, so what have you got to lose?

Throughout the ages, people have found different symbols to be lucky. Rabbit's feet, four-leaf clovers, and charms are all useful talismans. Fortuna isn't picky: if you have an object that brings you luck, no matter what it is, keep it with you. Fortuna thrives on belief, not skepticism, and carrying a tangi-

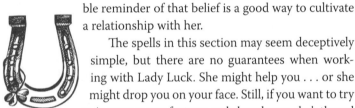

ble reminder of that belief is a good way to cultivate a relationship with her.

The spells in this section may seem deceptively simple, but there are no guarantees when working with Lady Luck. She might help you . . . or she might drop you on your face. Still, if you want to try to increase your fortune and abundance, she's the gal to talk to.

Fortuna is a great goddess to work with before a job interview, and she's also got the mojo you need to run into the right person at the right time. A word of warning: just because you find yourself in a patch of bad luck doesn't mean Fortuna is ignoring you. Bad luck balances good luck, and this goddess is all about spontaneous balance. What goes up must come down, but that also means that what's down won't stay that way forever.

SPELL FOR A JOB INTERVIEW

*Use this spell when you've already landed a job interview.
Fortuna will take care of the rest.*

YOU WILL NEED
- Closed-toe shoes
- A penny

1. As you get ready for the interview, set your shoes in front of your door, toes facing the door.

2. Set the penny inside the right shoe, face up. Say, *"Fortuna, favor me today. Let my footsteps bring me luck."*

3. Put on the shoes.

4. Walk with confidence into your interview. Know that whatever happens today, luck is on your side. If you don't get the job, it's a good thing, and if you do get the job, it's also a good thing.

5. When you get home from the interview, bury the penny in a potted plant or your backyard. Say, *"Fortuna favors me. I do not take luck when I do not need it. I know what I want, and I know how to get it."*

6. Repeat this spell whenever you have a job interview.

SPELL FOR A CHANCE MEETING

*Use this spell before you leave the house, and then keep your
eyes open for whomever Fortuna sends your way.*

YOU WILL NEED

- A green silk scarf or ribbon (long enough to wrap
  around your neck, hair, or wrist)
- A notebook

1. Hold the scarf or ribbon in both of your hands.

2. Say, *"Fortuna, there's someone I need to meet today. You
   know who it is: bring me face-to-face with this one."*

3. Tie the scarf around your neck, or, alternately, in your
   hair. If you are using a ribbon, you can wrap it around
   your wrist. Just make sure you tie it off in a double knot.

4. Keep the scarf on until you are home at the end of the
   day.

5. Take off the scarf. Say, *"Fortuna, you have favored me. Thanks for your attention."*

6. In your notebook, jot down a list of every person you encountered today. It may not be apparent whom you met because of the spell, but Fortuna doesn't always need to be seen to work. Know that whomever you encountered today was supposed to be there.

7. Repeat this spell whenever you are feeling lonely, or want to up your dating chances, or just when you want to open yourself up to making a new friend.

SPELL FOR GOOD LUCK

Whenever you want to increase the good fortune in your life, let Fortuna be your guide.

YOU WILL NEED

- Champagne
- Two glasses

1. Pop the champagne. Keep the cork in your coat pocket following this spell.

2. As you pour the first glass, say, *"Fortuna, I seek your smile. Bring good luck into my life."*

3. Pour the second glass. Say, *"Fortune favors me, and good luck bubbles inside of me. I am lucky."*

4. Clink the glasses together and say, *"Bon Fortuna!"*

5. Drink from the second glass, sipping and savoring the champagne. As the bubbles fill your nose, fantasize about the good luck you are seeking.

6. Leave the first glass out on the counter until you are done.

7. When you are finished with your glass, slowly dump the first glass down the drain.

8. This is always a good spell to do right before you have company over so you will have help finishing the bottle of champagne before it goes flat. Alternately, many stores now sell miniature bottles of champagne, which are perfect for performing this spell solo.

CHAPTER 6

Goddesses in Groups

The first time I ever did magic with a group of women was just like the night I turned twenty-one. I didn't know what I was doing, but I dove into the experience headfirst. The next morning, I had a pretty bad hangover. If you've never experienced a magical hangover, I hope you never will. It isn't fun. But a little bit of preparation can help you work magic in groups without suffering any ill effects.

Working magic alone can be exhilarating, but sometimes, you just want to hang out with your girlfriends. Most of the goddesses in this book are communal creatures, and they won't mind if you adapt the spells so that your friends can participate as well. But how do you go about setting up a goddess-centric gathering?

First, think about what you want to achieve. Are you hoping everyone will come together in a magical way with a shared intent, or do you just want to create safe space for your friends and loved ones to do whatever magic they choose? In my experience, unified gatherings work a lot better, but you can do whatever you want. You can write an elaborate ritual around the spell you want to use, or you can just throw everything together and see what happens. One key component to group magic is food: you know how your body responds to spell work, but you can't speak for everyone. Combining group magic with a potluck is one way to make sure that nobody suffers from a dreaded magical hangover. Plan your menu according to the gathering, and have fun!

Here are some suggestions for magical goddess gatherings.

Seasonal

SPRING

Get together with your girlfriends sometime in March to celebrate the season of rebirth and pretty flowers. Have everyone bring a fresh flower to the gathering, and serve light, brightly colored food.

Spells to consider for a springtime gathering include:

- Spell for Self-Awareness (chapter 1: Amaterasu)

- Spell for Tough Choices (chapter 2: Persephone)

- Spell for Mundane Magic (chapter 3: Brigid)

- Spell for Major Life Changes (chapter 4: Kali)

- Spell for Patience (chapter 5: Kuan Yin)

MIDSUMMER

In late June, have your friends meet in a public park or someone's large backyard. Bring a CD player or other musical device along, loaded with your favorite high-energy songs. Have a cookout, including corn on the cob.

Spells to consider for a midsummer gathering include:

- Spell to Increase Physical Energy (chapter 1: Sekhmet)

- Spell for a Strong Marriage (chapter 2: Hera)

- Spell for Safe Fun (chapter 3: Bast)

- Spell for Growth (chapter 4: Gaia)

- Spell for Prosperity (chapter 5: Lakshmi)

HARVEST

Sometime in October, get everyone together inside. Light candles instead of using electricity, and share a hearty meal. Have stews, chilies, breads, and casseroles on hand.

Spells to consider for a harvest gathering include:

- Spell to Spark Creativity (chapter 1: Sarasvati)

- Spell for Trust (chapter 2: Mary, Queen of Heaven)

- Spell for Fond Memories (chapter 3: Changing Woman)

- Spell for Choices (chapter 4: Hecate)

- Spell for Harvesting (chapter 5: Demeter)

WINTER

Just before the holidays in December, try to plan a quiet party with your girlfriends. Have everyone bring copies of a favorite family recipe to swap. Food for this gathering should be traditional American holiday fare: turkey and stuffing, mashed potatoes, and maybe even pumpkin pie.

Spells to consider for a winter gathering include:

- Spell for Clear Thinking (chapter 1: Athena)

- Spell for Family Balance (chapter 2: Persephone)

- Spell for Sacred Space (chapter 3: Hestia)

- Spell for Increased Awareness (chapter 4: Isis)

- Spell for Compassion (chapter 5: Kuan Yin)

Lunar

You can hold a gathering at any phase of the moon, but I'll give you two examples: a full moon gathering and a dark moon gathering. Focus on specific goddesses and choose your spells accordingly.

FULL MOON

Meet on the night of the full moon, or as close to it as possible. Have your friends bring only white food: champagne, fish, cream-based desserts, eggs, and bread are all options.

Goddesses to work with on the full moon:

- Sarasvati (chapter 1)

- Hera (chapter 2)

- Isis (chapter 4)

- Artemis (chapter 4)

- Kuan Yin (chapter 5)

DARK MOON

Get everyone together when the moon is no longer visible in the sky. For this gathering, serve only black or brown foods: dark chocolate, well-cooked meat, and whole wheat pasta are some suggestions.

Goddesses to work with on the dark moon:

- Oya (chapter 1)

- Persephone (chapter 2)

- Changing Woman (chapter 3)

- Kali (chapter 4)

- Hecate (chapter 4)

$\mathscr{S}olar$

Many of the goddesses in this book have a strong connection with solar energy. Have a party on a hot summer night and tap into their magic.

Goddess to work with for solar magic:

- Sekhmet (chapter 1)

- Amaterasu (chapter 1)

- Parvati (chapter 2)

- Bast (chapter 3)

- Brigid (chapter 3)

- Fortuna (chapter 5)

There are countless other ways to bring your friends together, and I hope you'll be creative as you plan magical gatherings. What about a birthday party with magical cake, or a baby shower with fairy dust in the air? The possibilities are limitless. Remember, the only ingredients for a good party are food and friends, but some goddesses and magical spells can't hurt, either!

CHAPTER 7

Attitude of Gratitude

Magic is so cool. It's still amazing to me that I can do a simple spell and see real results in my life. That can be a heady feeling, and it's easy to get swept up into an attitude of "me, me, me" when I'm doing magic. Let's be honest: we all want things to go our way, and magic can help us achieve our desires. But everything has to balance, and so I try to compensate for my magical demands with an attitude of gratitude.

While it can be exhilarating to work magic, you must proceed with caution: remember that the spells in this book derive their power from the different goddesses, and act accordingly. Mythology is rife with stories of the gruesome fates that await mortals who let their power and abilities go to their heads. There's Arachne, the arrogant weaver you've already heard about. She boasted of her prowess, and one day, Athena arrived to test the girl. Not only did Arachne dare to weave better than the goddess, she created a tapestry that showed Zeus as a rampant womanizer. Although this was true, Athena was certainly daddy's little girl, and she didn't take kindly to the insult. Arachne lived out the rest of her life as a spider to pay for her bad attitude.

Then there was Psyche. Although the girl wasn't guilty of anything other than being born beautiful, her parents loved to brag about their daughter. They even went so far as to claim that she was more beautiful than Aphrodite. Of course, this slander got back to the goddess, and Psyche was put through a series of miserable trials and tests before the goddess finally relented.

Perhaps the worst story of a mortal who doesn't know when to shut up is the tragic tale of Niobe. This mortal queen was blessed with many children, and she boasted that she was a better mother than Leto, the Titan who bore Artemis and Apollo. Niobe claimed that the number of children she had made her superior to the mother of the heavenly twins, but her boasts didn't last long. While her twin killed the sons, Artemis executed the daughters one by one, leaving Niobe bereft of her children. Sometimes, goddesses can be excessively cruel if they are offended.

There's a common theme in each of these stories, and one that we can hopefully learn from. Every time goddesses take action against mortals, it's because the mortals are arrogant. Arachne, Psyche, and Niobe were all blessed with talent, beauty, and wealth, but none of these women remembered to thank the goddesses for the good things in their lives. Their lack of gratitude destroyed them.

Luckily for us, it's easy to cultivate an attitude of gratitude, and you can even use magic to give thanks. Here are some ways you can incorporate magic into your thanksgiving, adding a bit more punch to your gratitude (and hopefully, these spells will help keep you on the good side of any given goddess!).

SPELL FOR SIMPLE THANKS

Use this spell to give thanks for anything, large or small.

YOU WILL NEED

- A bell (or wind chime)

1. Think about the thing you are thankful for. If there's a long list, that's awesome, but this spell works best if you concentrate on one thing at a time. (However, you can repeat this spell as many times as you want.)

2. Say, *"I am thankful for _____."*

3. Ring the bell three times.

4. Repeat steps 1 through 3 as many times as you wish.

SPELL FOR EXTENDED THANKS

Use this spell when you have a major thing to be thankful for, or when your list is exceptionally long.

YOU WILL NEED

- Pretty stationery (including an envelope)
- A blue, green, or purple pen

- A fire-safe container (or a fire pit)
- A wax seal (Optional: You can sometimes find sealing wax and seals at card stores and craft stores.)

1. Using the colored pen, begin writing a letter on the stationery. You can address a specific goddess, the universe at large, or, my favorite, yourself.

2. In the letter, explain in detail the thing(s) you are thankful for. Use all five of your senses in this description: sight, smell, taste, touch, and hearing.

3. After you have explained your thanks, seal the letter in the envelope. If you have a wax seal, you can use it; otherwise, seal the envelope with tape or a sticker.

4. Burn the letter. Watch the smoke rise into the air, and know that your thanks are going with it. Whoever needed to hear your heartfelt thanks will know what you said.

CANDLE SPELL FOR SIMPLE GRATITUDE

YOU WILL NEED

- A spell candle (any color)
- A specific goddess in mind

Whenever I work a spell and get immediate results, I light a candle just to thank the goddesses who helped me. I try to keep brightly colored spell candles on hand, and I pick one that's a color that particular goddess would like: red for Aphrodite, blue for Isis, purple for Hera, orange for Sekhmet, and so on. Then I light it and leave it burning until it extinguishes itself. Simple, right? You don't have to do anything special to prepare for this, but giving thanks is magic in and of itself. If you want, you can say thank you out loud to the goddess of your choice before you light the candle, but your intentions will be heard regardless.

SPELL FOR DEVOTION

Do you feel called to work with one goddess in particular? If you do, you might want to mark your devotion in a particular way. It's a great way to show your gratitude!

YOU WILL NEED

- A pencil
- Sketch paper
- Henna
- A safe, hygienic tattoo parlor (optional)

1. Using the sketch paper and the pencil, begin doodling. Think about the goddess you are honoring, and try to draw an image or symbol that makes you think of this goddess. (You can use actual symbols from art and architecture, or come up with something on your own.)

2. Once you have created an image that makes you think of the goddess, transfer the image to your skin, either using henna, or as a permanent tattoo.

3. If you choose henna, renew the image whenever it begins to fade.

4. Each morning, touch the image and say, *"Thank you, (goddess name), for this life."*

5. Each evening, touch the image and say, *"Thank you, (goddess name), for this day."*

Other Ways to Give Thanks

Even though this is a book of magic, there are plenty of mundane ways to cultivate an attitude of gratitude (and that don't involve a tattoo!). Here are some of my favorites:

- Schedule a monthly donation ($10 goes a long way!) to your local food pantry or shelter.

- Donate money to a group or organization in the name of your favorite goddess.

- Volunteer.

- Leave your change in a vending machine for the next person.

- Drop a penny (face up, of course!) in a public place: leave a little luck for the next person.

- Adopt a shelter pet.

- Campaign for a politician you believe in.

- Join your neighborhood watch or improvement committee.

- Invite friends over to dinner and cook for them.

- Treat a friend the next time you go out for coffee.

- In a drive-through, offer to pay the bill for the person behind you.

- Use your talents: if you're an artist, paint! If you're a singer, sing! If you're a scientist, invent! Don't be ashamed to give the world your gifts: you have them for a reason.

- Give away any coupons that you don't use to friends and family.

- Always tip 20 percent, no matter what.

- Donate books to your local school or library.

Magic is an amazing thing: it can brighten your life and magnify your happiness. Using the spells and suggestions in this section in addition to the individual spells listed in the rest of the book will make you even happier! Remember to cultivate an attitude of gratitude, and give thanks for the magic that surrounds you. And, here's a bonus: gratitude leads to abundance, so the more you give, the more you get. It's a win-win situation for everybody!

Basic Correspondences for the Spells in this Book

	Chapter 1: Health	Chapter 2: Relation-ships	Chapter 3: Home	Chapter 4: Travel and Protection	Chapter 5: Abundance
Goddesses	Athena Sekhmet Amaterasu Sarasvati Oya	Aphrodite Persephone Mary Hera Parvati	Brigid Hestia Juno Bast Changing Woman	Kali Isis Hecate Artemis Gaia	Lakshmi Kuan Yin Hathor Demeter Fortuna
Lunar Phases	Waxing Dark New	Full New	Waxing Full	Full Dark	Waxing Full
Elements and Cardi-nal Direc-tions	Air (East) Earth (North) Fire (South) Water (West)	Fire (South) Water (West) Earth (North)	Earth (North) Air (East)	Air (East) Fire (South)	Earth (North) Fire (South) Water (West)
Colors	White Yellow Blue Purple	Pink Red Green Gold	Green Yellow Brown	Blue Red Orange	Green Yellow Orange

REFERENCES

Adler, Margot. *Drawing Down the Moon.* 1979. Boston: Beacon Press.

Blake, Deborah. *The Goddess Is in the Details: Wisdom for the Everyday Witch.* 2010. Woodbury, MN: Llewellyn Publications.

Bradley, Kris. *Mrs. B's Guide to Household Witchery: Everyday Magic, Spells, and Recipes.* 2012. San Francisco: Weiser Books.

Budge, E. A. Wallis. *The Egyptian Book of the Dead: Revised Edition.* 2008. London: Penguin Books.

Conway, D. J. *Maiden, Mother, Crone.* 1994. Woodbury, MN: Llewellyn Publications.

———. *Moon Magick.* 1995. Woodbury, MN: Llewellyn Publications.

Coyle, T. Thorn. *Evolutionary Witchcraft.* 2005. New York: Tarcher.

Cunningham, Scott. *Cunningham's Encyclopedia of Magical Herbs.* 2009. Woodbury, MN: Llewellyn Publications.

———. *Wicca: A Guide for the Solitary Practitioner.* 1989. Woodbury, MN: Llewellyn Publications.

Curott, Phyllis. *Book of Shadows.* 1998. New York: Broadway Books.

———. *Witch Crafting.* 2001. New York: Broadway Books.

De Grandis, Francesca. *Be a Goddess!* 1998. San Francisco: Harper San Francisco.

———. *Goddess Initiation.* 2001. San Francisco: Harper San Francisco.

Dubats, Sally. *Natural Magick: The Essential Witch's Grimoire.* 1999. New York: Citadel Press.

Fortune, Dion. *Moon Magic.* 2003. San Francisco: Weiser Books.

———. *Sea Priestess.* 2003. San Francisco: Weiser Books.

Kant, Candace, and Anne Key (eds). *Heart of the Sun: An Anthology in Exaltation of Sekhmet.* 2011. Bloomington, IN: Goddess Ink.

Key, Anne. *Desert Priestess: A Memoir.* 2011. Bloomington, IN: Goddess Ink.

Monaghan, Patricia. *The Goddess Companion.* 2000. Minnesota: Llewellyn Publications.

———. *The Goddess Path.* 1999. Woodbury, MN: Llewellyn Publications.

———. *The New Book of Goddesses and Heroines.* 1981. Woodbury, MN: Llewellyn Publications.

Parnell, Pat. *Snake Woman and Other Explorations: Finding the Female in Divinity.* 2001. Portsmouth, NH: Peter E. Randall Publisher.

Reed, Ellen Cannon. *Circle of Isis: Ancient Egyptian Magic for Modern Witches.* 2002. Pompton Plains, NJ: New Page Books.

Reif, Jennifer. *Mysteries of Demeter: Rebirth of the Pagan Way.* 2000. San Francisco: Samuel Weiser.

Starhawk. *The Spiral Dance: A Rebirth of the Ancient Religion of the Great Goddess.* 1979. New York: HarperCollins.

Stone, Merlin. *Ancient Mirrors of Womanhood: A Treasury of Goddess and Heroine Lore from Around the World.* 1990. Boston: Beacon Press.

———. *When God Was a Woman.* 1976. San Diego: Harcourt Brace Jovanovich Publishers.

Straffon, Cheryl. *Daughters of the Earth: Goddess Wisdom for a Modern Age.* 2007. Winchester, UK: O Books.

Ward, Tim. *Savage Breast.* 2006. Winchester, UK: O Books.

ABOUT THE AUTHOR

Jen McConnel was born and raised in Michigan. She is a published poet and a writing instructor for her local community college. She is a devotee of Isis, but works closely with a number of goddesses. She's been published in *Sagewoman* and *PanGaia*, and she blogs at Witches and Pagans and Patheos. She lives in North Carolina with her husband and their cats.

Visit her online at *www.jenmcconnel.com.*